SKILLS
BASE
GEOGRAPHY

KEITH GRIMWADE
AND GREG HART

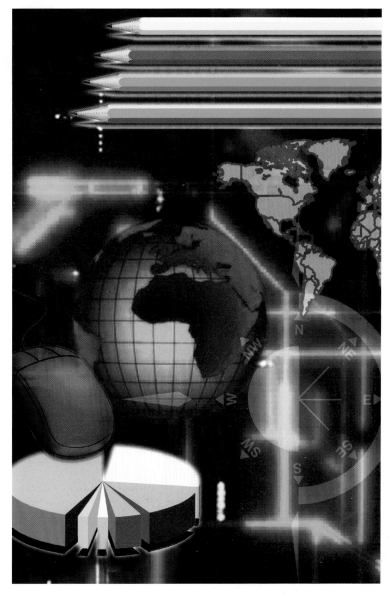

Hodder & Stoughton
A MEMBER OF THE HODDER HEADLINE GROUP

GW01035962

Acknowledgements

The publishers would like to thank the following for giving permission to reproduce copyright photographs in this book:

Science Photo Library, Figures 2.26, 5.16, 5.18, 5.19, 5.20, 5.21, 5.22, 5.23; Sealand, Figures 3.27, 5.3, 5.9; Photoair, Figures 5.6, 5,7.

All other photos are supplied by the authors.

Maps reproduced from the Ordnance Survey Mapping with the permission of the Controller of Her Majesty's Stationery Office © Crown copyright; Licence number 399450.

Every effort has been made to contact the holders of copyright material used in this book, but if any have been overlooked, the publishers will be pleased to make the necessary alterations at the first opportunity.

Icons for links to themes

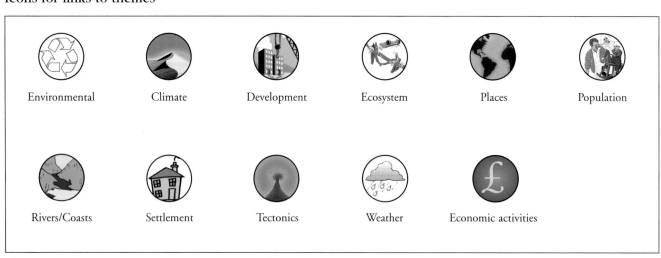

Environmental   Climate   Development   Ecosystem   Places   Population

Rivers/Coasts   Settlement   Tectonics   Weather   Economic activities

Photocopiable graph and map outlines for the workshop activities in this book are available in the Skills Base Geography Resource Pack (ISBN: 0340 67019 3)

Orders: please contact Bookpoint Ltd., 39 Milton Park, Abingdon, Oxon OX14 4TD. Telephone (44) 01235 400414, Fax (44) 01235 400454. Lines are open from 9.00–6.00, Monday to Saturday, with a 24 hour message answering service. E-mail address: orders@bookpoint.co.uk

British Library Cataloguing in Publication Data
A catalogue record for this title is available from The British Library

ISBN 0 340 67020 7

First published 1999
Impression number   10 9 8 7 6 5 4 3 2 1
Year   2004 2003 2002 2001 2000 1999

Copyright © 1999

Typeset and designed by Liz Rowe

Printed in Hong Kong for Hodder & Stoughton Educational, a division of Hodder Headline Plc, 338 Euston Road, London NW1 3BH by Colorcraft Ltd.

Contents

CHAPTER 1

Graphs

1.1 *Bar graphs*

Bar charts

Introduction

A bar chart is made up of columns. Each column shows the number of something. For example, Figure 1.1 shows the number of pupils in a class survey who came to school by car, by bus, by bike, by walking and by other means of transport, e.g. by taxi. A bar chart could also be used to show the amount of rain in each month of a year, or the number of different types of shop in a town.

FIGURE 1.1 *How to draw a bar chart*

④ Add a title.

③ The height of the bar shows the number it represents.

① Draw the scale for the y axis. This shows the number.

② Mark off and label a place for each bar on the x axis. This shows the groups.

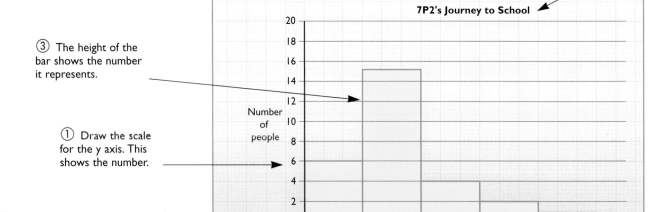

FIGURE 1.2 *Environment Survey Class 7P2 June 1996*

1 How do you usually get to school?

Method	Car	Walk	Bus	Bike	Other
No. of pupils	6	2	15	4	1

2 How many of your families recycle?

Paper	Clothes	Glass	Metal	Plastic
18	12	18	4	2

3 How many of your houses have?

Loft insulation	Double glazing	Energy saving light bulbs	Cavity wall insulation	An insulating jacket on the hot water cylinder
20	16	4	6	28

1 Make a copy of the bar chart outline in Figure 1.3. Use it to show the results about **recycling** from the class survey (Figure 1.2).
2 a) Which materials are recycled the most?
   b) Why do you think this is the case?
3 Which material is recycled the least? Suggest why this is the case.
4 Draw a bar chart to show the results about **insulation** from the class survey (Figure 1.2).
5 Why do you think so few families use energy saving light bulbs?

FIGURE 1.3   *Bar chart outline for question 1*

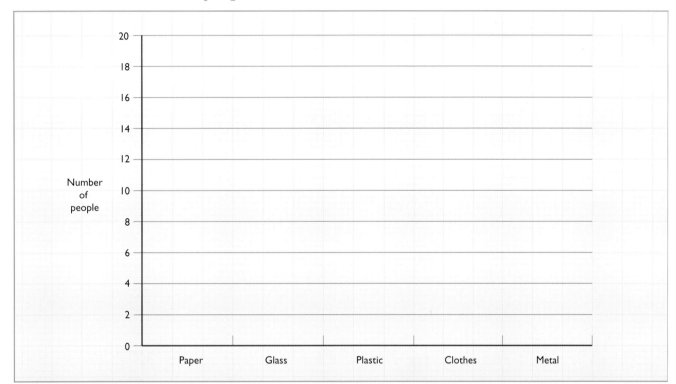

WORD BOX

insulation something that stops heat escaping; e.g. a layer of glass fibre in the loft, polystyrene injected into the cavity (gap) between the inside and outside walls of a house, foam jackets on hot water cylinders
recycling using waste to remake something rather than throwing it away

Comparative bar graphs

Introduction

Comparative bar graphs are drawn in a similar way to bar charts but the columns are put next to each other so that it is easy to see the similarities and differences between them. For example, Figure 1.4 shows changes in the area of **green belt** between 1979 and 1989 in four regions of England. It is easy to see that the amount of green belt in each of these regions increased between the two years. Another use for a comparative bar graph would be to show changes in the exports of different goods between two years.

FIGURE 1.4   *How to draw a comparative bar chart*

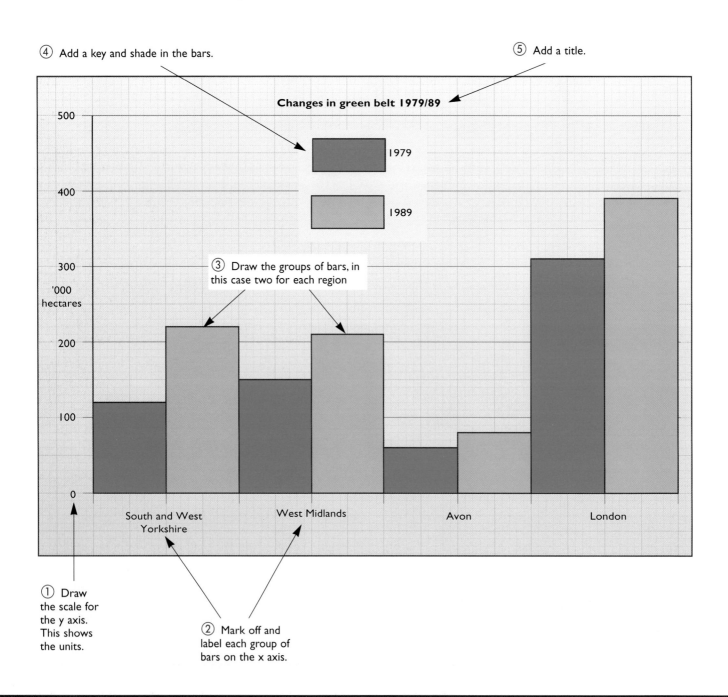

④ Add a key and shade in the bars.

⑤ Add a title.

Changes in green belt 1979/89

1979

1989

③ Draw the groups of bars, in this case two for each region

'000 hectares

500

400

300

200

100

0

South and West Yorkshire

West Midlands

Avon

London

① Draw the scale for the y axis. This shows the units.

② Mark off and label each group of bars on the x axis.

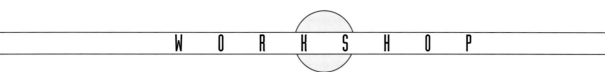
W O R K S H O P

1 (You will need a copy of Figure 1.5 for this activity.) Draw a comparative bar graph to show the statistics in Figure 1.6. Each country should have four columns, one for each type of land use. Each different land use should be a different colour.

2 What are the main differences shown on your graph?

3 Suggest reasons for these differences.

W O R D   B O X

green belt   a ring of land surrounding a town or city upon which no new building is allowed

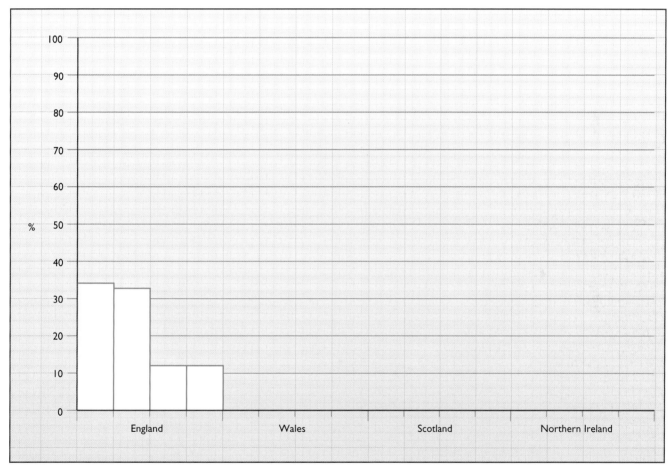

FIGURE 1.5   *Graph outline for question 1*

FIGURE 1.6   *Land use in the UK, 1996 (%)*
Source: Geographical Association's Land Use – UK survey

	ARABLE	GRASS	WOODLAND AND SHRUB	BUILT-UP
ENGLAND	34	33	12	12
WALES	9	54	13	8
SCOTLAND	10	29	18	4
NORTHERN IRELAND	5	61	3	6

Compound bar graphs

Introduction

A compound bar graph can be used if you want to show how a total is divided up and how it varies from place to place, or year to year. The length of the bar represents the total value, which can be either a real number or a percentage. The component parts show how the total value is divided up. For example, Figure 1.7 shows not only how world energy consumption has changed over a 20-year period but also how different regions have accounted for this change. A compound bar graph could also be used to show how total employment is divided up between men and women and how this varies from year to year.

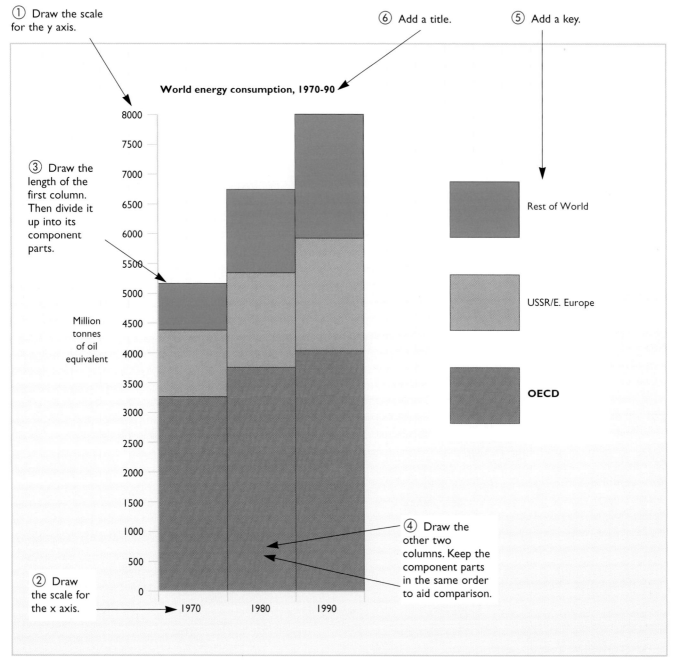

① Draw the scale for the y axis.

⑥ Add a title.

⑤ Add a key.

World energy consumption, 1970-90

③ Draw the length of the first column. Then divide it up into its component parts.

Rest of World

USSR/E. Europe

OECD

Million tonnes of oil equivalent

④ Draw the other two columns. Keep the component parts in the same order to aid comparison.

② Draw the scale for the x axis.

1970   1980   1990

FIGURE 1.7   *How to draw a compound bar graph*

W O R K S H O P

1 (You will need a copy of Figure 1.8 for this activity.) Draw a compound bar graph to show the statistics in Figure 1.9.
2 What are the main trends shown on your graph?
3 Do any of these trends surprise you? Why?
4 Try to explain these trends.
5 Use the statistics in Figure 1.10 to draw a compound bar graph to show oil production between 1970 and 1990.
6 What are the main changes shown on your graph?
7 Can you suggest reasons for these changes?

	1985	1990	2005	2020
COAL	32	33	30	34
OIL	36	34	33	32
NATURAL GAS	24	23	27	28
NUCLEAR	7	7	7	4
HEP/RENEWABLES	1	3	3	2

FIGURE 1.9 *Sources of energy in the UK, 1985–2020 (%)*

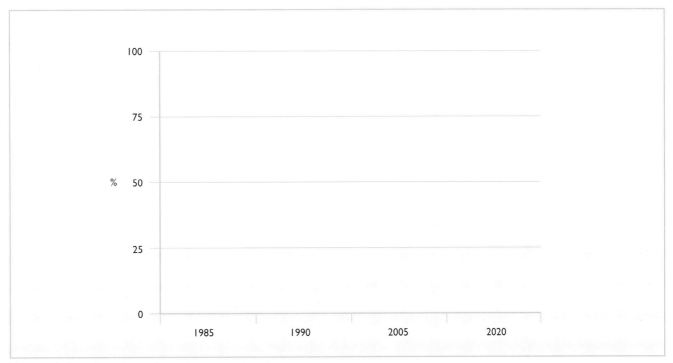

FIGURE 1.8 *Graph outline for question 1*

	1970	1975	1980	1985	1990
ASIA AND AUSTRALASIA	2	3	5	6	7
AFRICA	6	5	6	5	7
MIDDLE EAST	14	19	18	11	16
NON-OECD EUROPE	7	10	12	12	11
OECD EUROPE	1	1	2	4	4
LATIN AMERICA	5	4	6	6	7
NORTH AMERICA	12	11	11	12	10

FIGURE 1.10 *Oil production by area (million barrels daily)*

W O R D   B O X

OECD Organisation for Economic Co-operation and Development: an organisation of 24 of the world's More Economically Developed Countries (MEDCs)

1.2 *Line graphs* £

Simple line graphs

Introduction

A simple line graph shows how one **variable** changes against another. For example, Figure 1.11 shows how population changes against time. The variables must have something to do with each other. Two examples are population which changes from year to year and temperature which changes with height.

FIGURE 1.11 *How to draw a simple line graph*

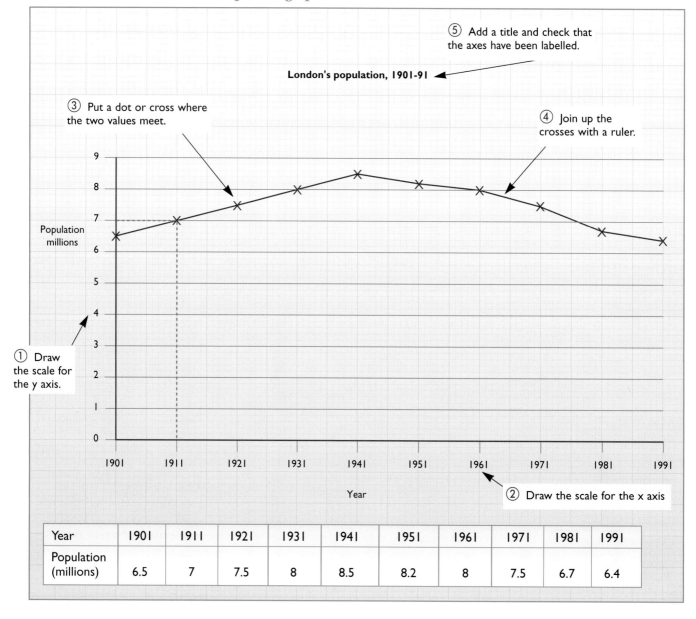

Year	1901	1911	1921	1931	1941	1951	1961	1971	1981	1991
Population (millions)	6.5	7	7.5	8	8.5	8.2	8	7.5	6.7	6.4

1 (You will need a copy of the graph outline in Figure 1.12.) Plot the statistics in Figure 1.13 to show population growth in East Anglia, as a line graph.

2 Describe what your graph shows.

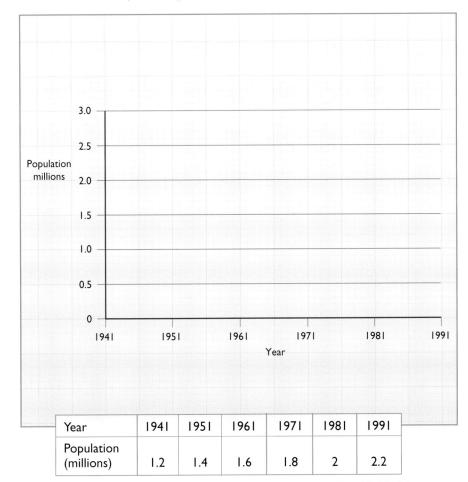

FIGURE **1.12** *Graph outline for question 1*

Year	1941	1951	1961	1971	1981	1991
Population (millions)	1.2	1.4	1.6	1.8	2	2.2

FIGURE **1.13** *Population growth in East Anglia, 1941–91*

3 Use the statistics in Figure 1.14 to draw a line graph to show population growth in the UK, 1901–91. The y axis should go from 0 to 60 million in "5 million" steps. The x axis should go from 1901 to 1991 in 10-year intervals.

4 Describe what your graph shows.

variable a value that goes up or down on a continuous scale, e.g. population, years, temperature, height

FIGURE **1.14** *Population growth in the UK, 1901–91*

Year	1901	1911	1921	1931	1941	1951	1961	1971	1981	1991
Population (millions)	38	42	44	46	48	51	53	56	56	57

Comparative line graphs

Introduction

A comparative line graph has more than one line drawn on the same graph outline. For example, Figure 1.15 shows the UK's changing **occupational structure** - the percentage of people employed in primary, secondary and tertiary industry - on the one graph. There are many other uses for this technique, e.g. to show the changing populations of the main towns of a country. However, it is important not to have too many lines or the graph becomes difficult to read.

⑤ Add a title and check that both axes have been labelled.

① Draw the scale for the y axis.

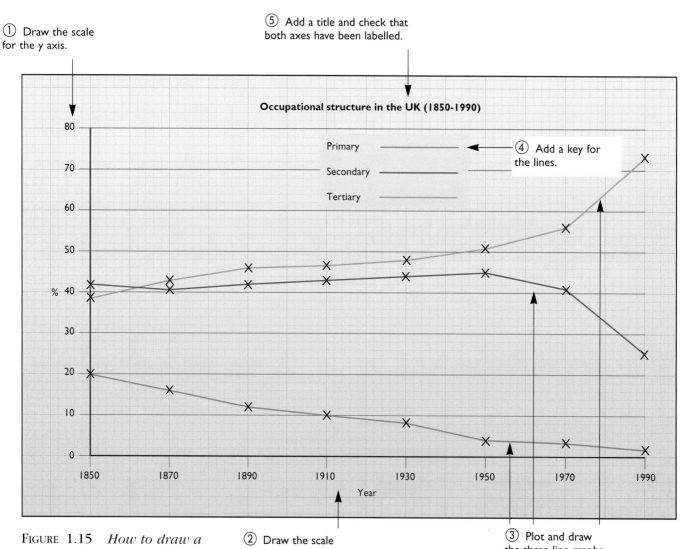

④ Add a key for the lines.

③ Plot and draw the three line graphs.

② Draw the scale for the x axis.

FIGURE 1.15 *How to draw a comparative line graph*

Year	1850	1870	1890	1910	1930	1950	1970	1990
Primary %	20	16	12	10	8	4	3	2
Secondary %	42	41	42	43	44	45	41	25
Tertiary %	38	43	46	47	48	51	56	73

CHAPTER 1

WORKSHOP

1 (You will need a copy of the graph outline in Figure 1.16 for this activity.) Plot the statistics in Figure 1.17 to show crop production in the UK as a comparative line graph.
2 Describe what your graph shows.
3 Suggest reasons for the changes shown on your graph.
4 Use the statistics in Figure 1.18 to draw a comparative line graph to show the changing mix of energy in the UK, 1957-95.
5 Describe the changes shown on your graph.
6 Suggest reasons for these changes.

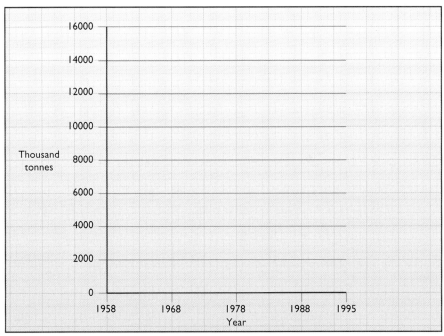

FIGURE 1.16 *Graph outline for question 1*

	1958	1968	1978	1988	1995
Barley	8221	8270	9848	8879	6833
Wheat	2755	3469	6613	11 605	14 310
Sugar beet	5835	7119	6382	7980	8431
Potatoes	5646	6872	7331	6000	6396
N.B. All figures are in thousand tonnes					

FIGURE 1.17 *Crop production in the UK*

	COAL	OIL	NATURAL GAS	OTHERS
1957	85	15	0	0
1967	59	39	1	1
1977	38	41	19	2
1987	33	37	24	6
1995	20	42	29	9

FIGURE 1.18 *The UK's changing energy mix, 1957-95*

occupational structure the balance between the different categories of industry: primary (the getting of raw materials); secondary (manufacturing); and tertiary (services)

Compound line graphs

Introduction

A compound line graph shows both the individual and the **component parts** of a total. For example, Figure 1.19 shows that the total value of the UK's exports was £47 290 million in 1980 and £103 720 million in 1990 (the top line); and that the value of the UK's exports to the EU in 1980 was £21 600 million (the difference between the top of the EU portion of the graph and the bottom of the EU portion of the graph, i.e. 47 290 − 25 690 = 21 600).

FIGURE 1.19 *How to draw a compound line graph*

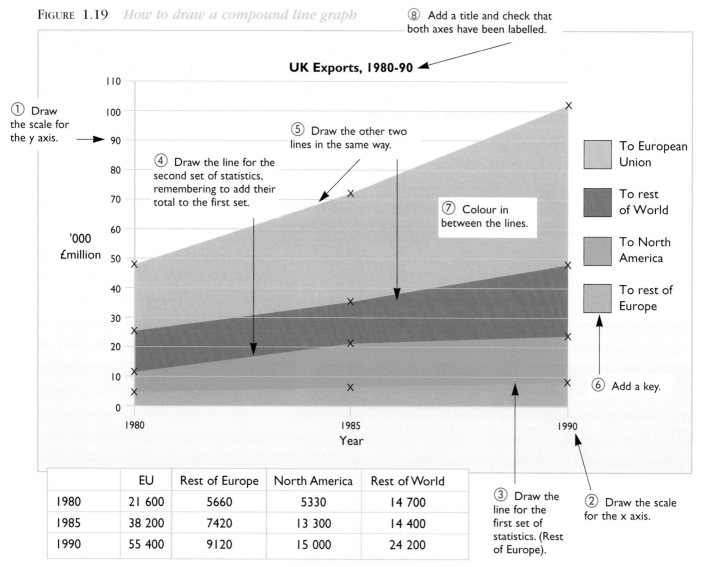

	EU	Rest of Europe	North America	Rest of World
1980	21 600	5660	5330	14 700
1985	38 200	7420	13 300	14 400
1990	55 400	9120	15 000	24 200

N.B. All figures are in £ million

You can use this type of graph when you have data that can be presented as line graphs. However, the statistics must have something in common. For example, in Figure 1.19 it is the UK's trade with the rest of the world, while in Figure 1.21 it is the world production of cereal crops.

This is a difficult type of line graph to draw but it is an excellent way of presenting certain types of data because it draws attention to what at first can seem like a complicated set of statistics.

FIGURE 1.20   *Graph outline for question 1*

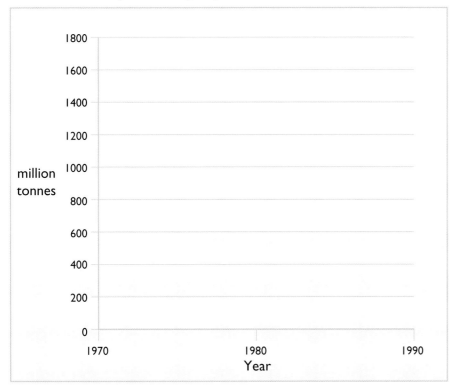

1 (You will need a copy of the graph outline in Figure 1.20 for this activity.) Plot the statistics in Figure 1.21 to show world production of cereal crops, as a compound line graph.
2 Describe and explain what your graph shows.

	1970	1980	1990
wheat	300 000	400 000	600 000
rice	300 000	400 000	500 000
maize	300 000	400 000	500 000

FIGURE 1.21   *World production of cereal crops, 1970–90 (thousand tonnes)*

3 Use the statistics in Figure 1.22 to draw a compound line graph to show world production of important raw materials, 1970–90.
4 Describe and explain what your graph shows.

FIGURE 1.22   *World production of important raw materials, 1970–90 (thousand tonnes)*

	1970	1980	1990
copper ore	6320	7900	9040
lead ore	3400	3600	3345
asbestos	4682	4700	3980

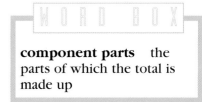

W O R D   B O X

component parts   the parts of which the total is made up

1.3 *Pie charts 1*

Introduction

A pie chart is a good way of showing how a total is divided up. For example, it is easy to see from Figure 1.23 that most people in Huntingdon work in **tertiary industry**. Also, by looking at the scale you can work out the percentages for each sector. For example, in Figure 1.23 you can work out that 1 per cent work in **primary industry**, 33 per cent in **secondary industry** and 66 per cent in **tertiary industry**. Pie charts have many other uses, e.g. to show how the land use of an area is divided up, or to show how the atmosphere is divided up between different gases.

FIGURE 1.23 *How to draw a simple pie chart*

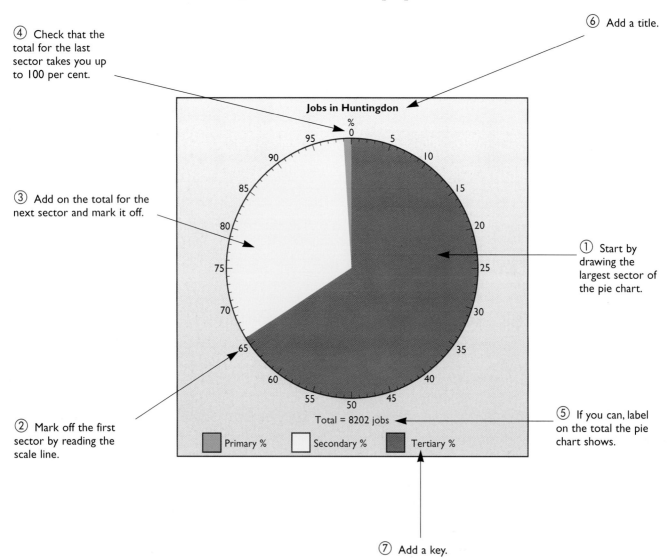

④ Check that the total for the last sector takes you up to 100 per cent.

⑥ Add a title.

③ Add on the total for the next sector and mark it off.

① Start by drawing the largest sector of the pie chart.

⑤ If you can, label on the total the pie chart shows.

② Mark off the first sector by reading the scale line.

Jobs in Huntingdon

Total = 8202 jobs

Primary %   Secondary %   Tertiary %

⑦ Add a key.

1 (You will need two copies of the pie chart outline, Figure 1.25, for this activity.) Use the statistics in Figure 1.24 to draw pie charts to show the jobs people do in (a) East Anglia and (b) London and the south east.

2 What differences can you see between the two pie charts?
3 Can you think of any reasons for these differences?

FIGURE 1.24 *Comparing jobs*

	EAST ANGLIA	LONDON and the SOUTH EAST
PRIMARY %	5	2
SECONDARY %	29	25
TERTIARY %	66	73

primary industry   the getting of raw materials
secondary industry   this is manufacturing (making) things out of raw materials
tertiary industry   people in this type of industry provide a service, e.g. an office worker, a fire fighter, a shop assistant

FIGURE 1.25 *Pie chart outline*

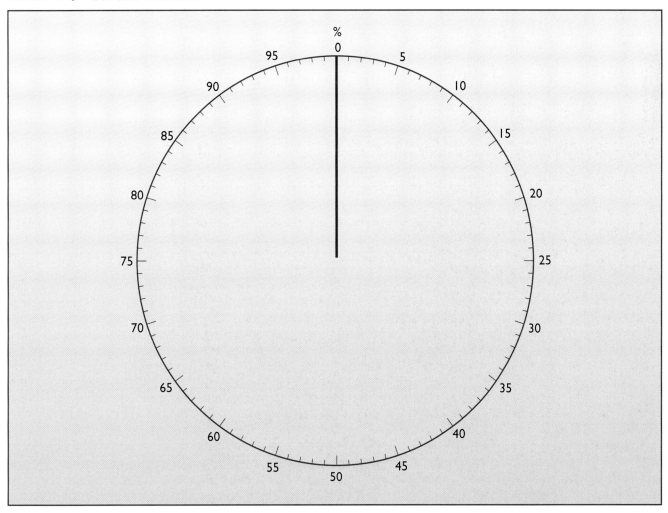

Pie charts 2

Introduction

A pie chart can be drawn from raw data, not just from percentages, as long as some simple rules are followed. You can use this technique whenever you want to show how a total is divided up. The first stage is to fill in a pie chart table (Figure 1.26): a pocket calculator will help with this. The second stage is to draw the pie chart itself: you could use the pie chart outline (see Figure 1.24, page 15), or a compass and protractor (Figure 1.27).

FIGURE 1.26 *An example of a pie chart table*

① Work out the figures for this column by dividing the number of households in each category by the total number of households and multiplying by 100.

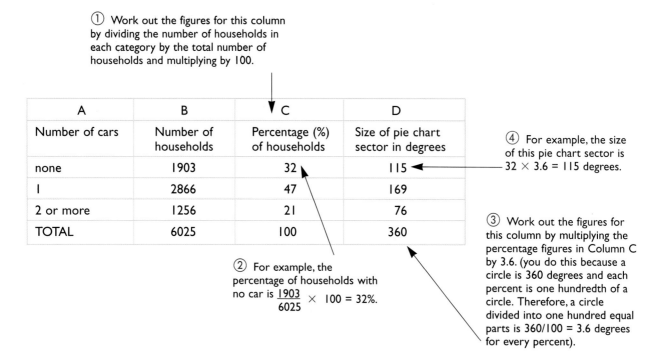

A	B	C	D
Number of cars	Number of households	Percentage (%) of households	Size of pie chart sector in degrees
none	1903	32	115
I	2866	47	169
2 or more	1256	21	76
TOTAL	6025	100	360

④ For example, the size of this pie chart sector is 32 × 3.6 = 115 degrees.

② For example, the percentage of households with no car is $\frac{1903}{6025}$ × 100 = 32%.

③ Work out the figures for this column by multiplying the percentage figures in Column C by 3.6. (you do this because a circle is 360 degrees and each percent is one hundredth of a circle. Therefore, a circle divided into one hundred equal parts is 360/100 = 3.6 degrees for every percent).

FIGURE 1.27 *Drawing the pie chart*

① Draw the circle with a compass.

② Draw the '12 o'clock' **radius** as the start point for the first sector.

③ Measure the angles with a protractor.

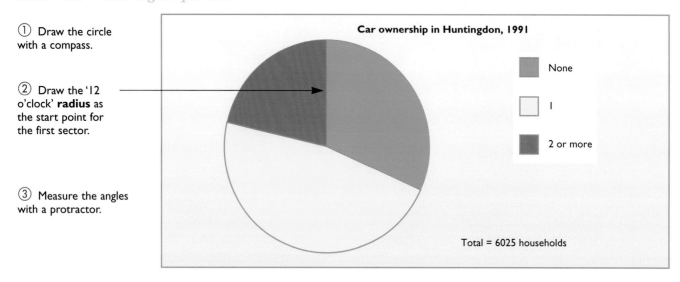

Car ownership in Huntingdon, 1991

None

I

2 or more

Total = 6025 households

CHAPTER 1

W O R K S H O P

FIGURE 1.28   *Brampton statistics: car ownership*

Number of cars	Number of households	Percentage (%) of households	Size of pie chart sector in degrees
none	282		
1	880		
2 or more	532		
TOTAL			

FIGURE 1.29   *Brampton statistics: type of house*

Type of house	Number of houses	Percentage (%) of houses	Size of pie chart sector in degrees
Detached	716		
Semi-detached	703		
Terraced	229		
Flat	151		
TOTAL			

W O R D   B O X

detached   a house by itself
flat   a building divided up into two or more households
radius   a straight line from the centre to the edge of a circle
semi-detached   a house which is joined to another
terraced   three or more houses joined together

1   Draw pie charts to show the data in Figures 1.28 and 1.29 about Brampton, a village in Cambridgeshire.
2   Describe what each of your pie charts tells us about Brampton.
3   Compare Figure 1.27 with the pie chart you have drawn for the statistics in Figure 1.28. Suggest two possible reasons that could explain the differences between these two pie charts.

1.4 Wind roses

Wind roses 1

Introduction

A wind rose shows wind directions for a place. For example, Figure 1.30 shows the wind directions for Huntingdon in July 1994. You can easily see the **prevailing wind direction**. This is useful information because different winds bring different types of weather.

FIGURE 1.30 *How to draw a simple wind rose*

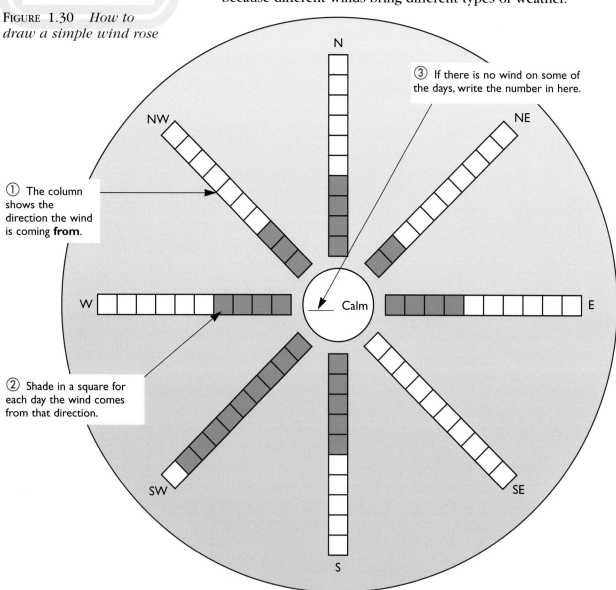

③ If there is no wind on some of the days, write the number in here.

① The column shows the direction the wind is coming **from**.

② Shade in a square for each day the wind comes from that direction.

Calm

DIRECTION	N	NE	E	SE	S	SW	W	NW	CALM
NUMBER OF DAYS	4	2	4	0	5	9	4	3	0

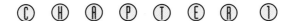

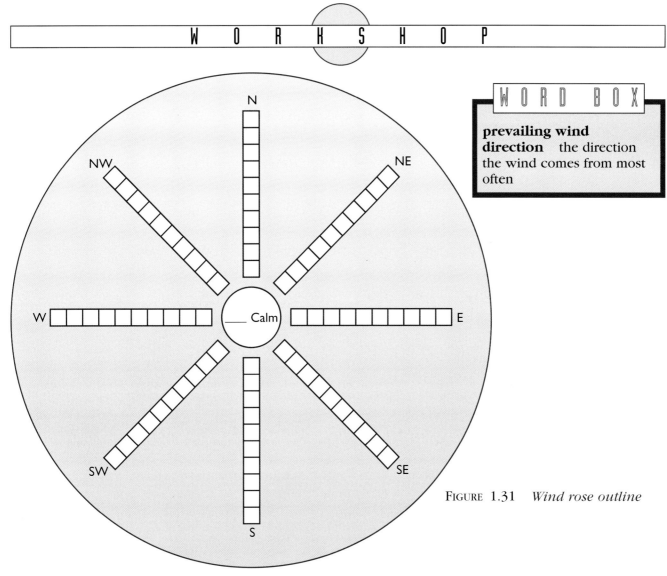

WORD BOX

prevailing wind direction the direction the wind comes from most often

FIGURE 1.31 *Wind rose outline*

1 (You will need a copy of the wind rose outline in Figure 1.31 for this activity.) Plot the statistics in Figure 1.32 to show wind directions for Huntingdon in the month of August 1994.
2 What was the prevailing wind direction in August?
3 Where was the prevailing wind coming from in July: across the continent of Europe or the Atlantic Ocean? (Look back at Figure 1.30 and use an atlas to help you.)
4 Where was the prevailing wind coming from in August: the continent of Europe or the Atlantic Ocean?

FIGURE 1.32 *Wind direction for Huntingdon, August 1994*

DIRECTION	N	NE	E	SE	S	SW	W	NW	CALM
NUMBER OF DAYS	1	2	5	10	3	2	3	2	3

5 Use your answers to questions 3 and 4 to explain why July was wetter than August.

Compound wind roses

Introduction

A compound wind rose shows wind strength as well as wind direction, e.g. Figure 1.33 shows the wind strength and direction for Huntingdon in July 1994. This extra information is useful because wind strength is an important aspect of the weather – it can feel chilly even on a warm day if the wind is very strong. It is also interesting to look at the relationship between wind strength and direction – are the winds from some directions always stronger than others?

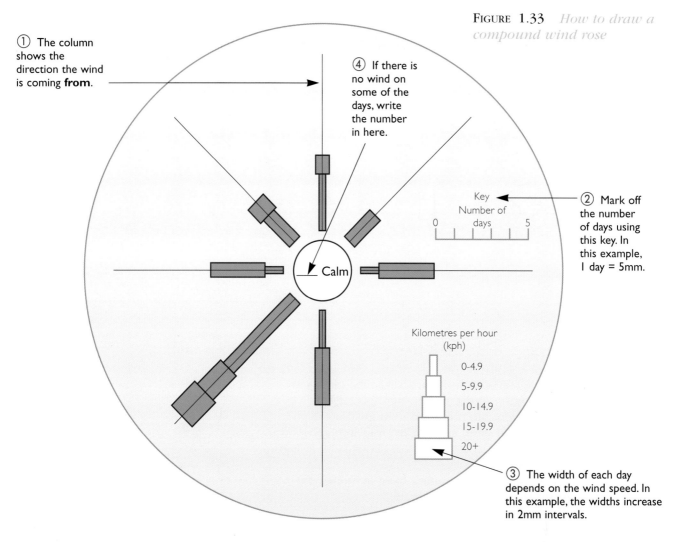

FIGURE 1.33 *How to draw a compound wind rose*

① The column shows the direction the wind is coming **from**.

④ If there is no wind on some of the days, write the number in here.

Key
Number of days
0   5

② Mark off the number of days using this key. In this example, 1 day = 5mm.

Calm

Kilometres per hour (kph)

0-4.9
5-9.9
10-14.9
15-19.9
20+

③ The width of each day depends on the wind speed. In this example, the widths increase in 2mm intervals.

WIND STRENGTH IN KPH	N	NE	E	SE	S	SW	W	NW	CALM
0 – 4.9	3		1		2		1		
5 – 9.9	1	2	3		3	5	3	2	
10 – 14.9						2		1	
15 – 19.9						2			
20+									

1 (You will need a copy of the compound wind rose outline in Figure 1.34 for this activity.) Use the statistics in Figure 1.35 to show wind strength and direction for Huntingdon in August 1994. You will first have to construct a **frequency table** like the one in Figure 1.33.

FIGURE 1.34 *Compound wind rose outline*

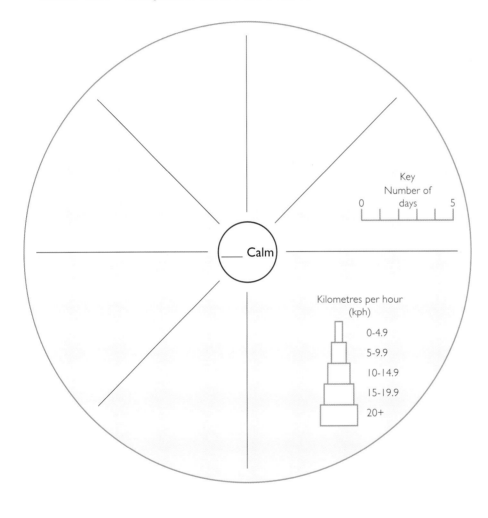

FIGURE 1.35 *Wind speed and direction for Huntingdon, August 1994*

DATE	WIND SPEED (KPH)	WIND DIRECTION
1	8	N
2	16	NW
3	12	NW
4	3	SE
5	2	SE
6	2	S
7	2	SE
8	2	S
9	2	S
10	0	C
11	0	C
12	0	C
13	12	W
14	14	W
15	22	W
16	16	SW
17	18	SW
18	6	SE
19	7	SE
20	4	SE
21	6	E
22	4	E
23	8	SE
24	14	E
25	10	E
26	12	E
27	12	SE
28	14	SE
29	14	SE
30	8	NE
31	8	NE

W O R D   B O X

frequency table   a table of statistics that shows how often certain things occur

2 Is there a relationship between wind strength and direction?
3 How do you think wind strength would have affected weather?

1.5 *Scatter graphs*

Scatter graphs 1

Introduction

A scatter graph shows the relationship between two **variables**. For example, Figure 1.36 shows that **infant mortality** is higher in the countries that have a lower income. This is what you would expect because poor countries have less money to spend on medical care than rich countries. The Workshop on page 23 gives other uses for this technique. It could also be used in physical geography, e.g. to show the relationship between height and temperature.

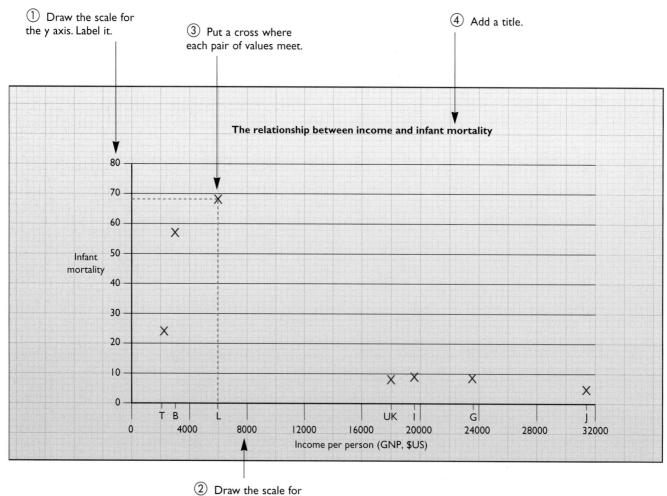

① Draw the scale for the y axis. Label it.

③ Put a cross where each pair of values meet.

④ Add a title.

The relationship between income and infant mortality

② Draw the scale for the x axis. Label it.

FIGURE 1.36 *How to draw a scatter graph*

1 (You will need a copy of the scatter graph outline, Figure 1.37, for this question.) Use the statistics in Figure 1.38 to draw a scatter graph to show the relationship between income and energy used per person.
2 What relationship does your graph show?
3 What do you think could explain this relationship?

infant mortality the number of babies who die before they are one year old, for every 1000 babies that are born
variable a value that goes up or down on a continuous scale, e.g. population, years, temperature, height

FIGURE 1.37 *Scatter graph outline*

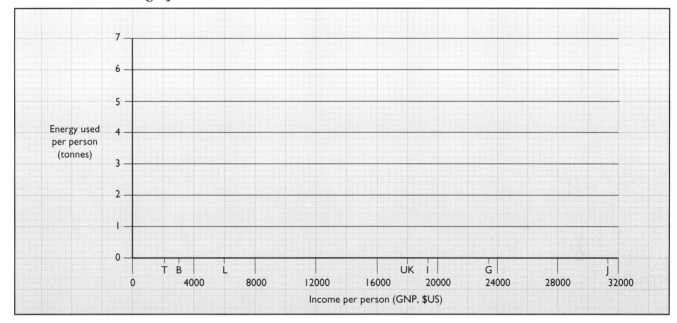

4 Use the statistics in Figure 1.38 to draw a scatter graph to show the relationship between income per year and percentage of workers employed in farming.
5 What relationship does your graph show?
6 What do you think could explain this relationship?

FIGURE 1.38 *Scatter graph statistics*

	INCOME PER PERSON (GNP 1993 $ US)	INFANT MORTALITY (1990-95)	YEARLY ENERGY USED PER PERSON (TONNES 1992)	% OF WORKERS EMPLOYED IN FARMING 1993
JAPAN	31450	5	4.74	6
GERMANY	23560	8	5.89	4
UK	17970	8	5.4	2
ITALY	19620	9	4.02	6
LIBYA	6500	68	3.46	13
BRAZIL	3020	57	0.81	23
THAILAND	2040	24	0.89	62

Scatter graphs 2

Introduction

A good way of seeing if there is a relationship between the two variables on a scatter graph is to draw on a best fit line. This is a line that comes as close to as many of the points on the graph as possible. The main types of relationship are shown in Figure 1.39. Of course, a correlation between the two variables does not mean that one causes the other; e.g. there is a **correlation** between the sale of barbecues and the sale of ice creams, but the cause of both is the weather!

FIGURE 1.39 *The relationship between two variables*

① **Positive correlation** As one variable increases (the x axis), so does the other, e.g. as Gross National Product (GNP) increases, so does use of energy.

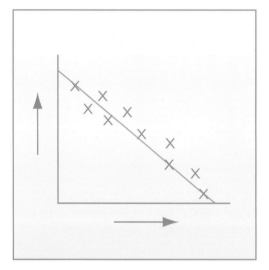

② **Negative correlation** As one variable increases (the x axis), the other decreases, e.g. as GNP increases, infant mortality decreases.

③ **Perfect correlation** All the points lie on the line of best fit. You can have a perfect positive correlation, as in this example, or a perfect negative correlation.

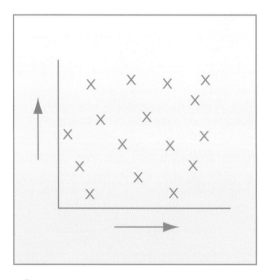

④ **No correlation** If the points are scattered and it seems impossible to draw on a line of best fit, it almost certainly means there is no correlation between the two variables.

You will need three copies of the scatter graph outline, Figure 1.40, for the tasks in this workshop. The x axis has been drawn for you but in each case you will have to work out the scale for the y axis yourself. Figure 1.41 shows the results of a river study carried out by Year 11 students. They recorded information about a local river at various places along its course. They started close to its source and visited ten sites, the last one being six and a half kilometres downstream. They used scatter graphs to present and to analyse the results. This allowed them to answer some important geographical questions. The tasks in this workshop ask you to present and to analyse the statistics in the same way that they did.

FIGURE 1.40   *Scatter graph outline for question 1*

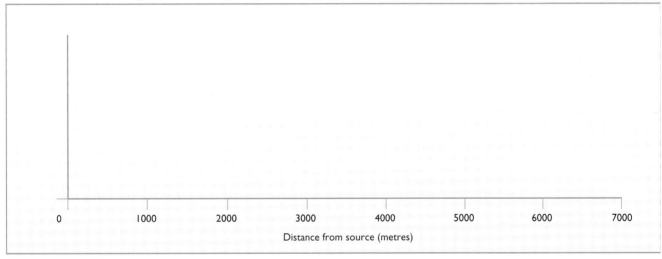

Carry out points (a)–(d) for each of the following three questions:

1 Is there a relationship between distance from **source** and average speed?
2 Does a relationship exist between distance from **source** and **discharge**?
3 Does a relationship exist between distance from source and **bedload**?
   a) Plot a scatter graph to show the relationship between the two variables.
   b) Draw on a line of best fit.
   c) Describe the relationship.
   d) Suggest some reasons for the relationship.

W O R D   B O X

bedload   material moved along the bottom of a river
correlation   the relationship between two variables
discharge   the volume of water flowing past a certain point in a river measured in cumecs (cubic metres per second)
source   the beginning of a river

FIGURE 1.41   *River survey statistics*

SITE	1	2	3	4	5	6	7	8	9	10
DISTANCE FROM SOURCE (metres)	200	1100	1900	2400	3100	3900	4200	5300	5900	6500
AVERAGE SPEED (METRES/SECOND)	0.78	0.62	0.54	0.91	0.89	0.99	1.2	1.34	1.21	1.45
DISCHARGE (CUMECS)	0.09	0.21	0.26	0.46	0.55	1.19	1.74	2.09	1.89	2.74
BEDLOAD SIZE (average pebble length, mm)	289	198	201	189	134	145	101	86	92	67

1.6 *Special graphs* £

Pictograms

Introduction

A pictogram uses **symbols** to show the statistics you want to present. Each symbol stands for a certain amount, e.g. in Figure 1.42 each symbol represents 2 million cars. Figure 1.43 shows how the number of symbols was worked out. You can use pictograms to present many types of data, e.g. the number of volcanoes, or the number of people, in a country. Pictograms can look really good, but deciding on the amount each symbol stands for can be difficult because 'real' statistics have been rounded up or down to give whole numbers so that the map is easier to draw.

FIGURE 1.42 *How to draw a pictogram*

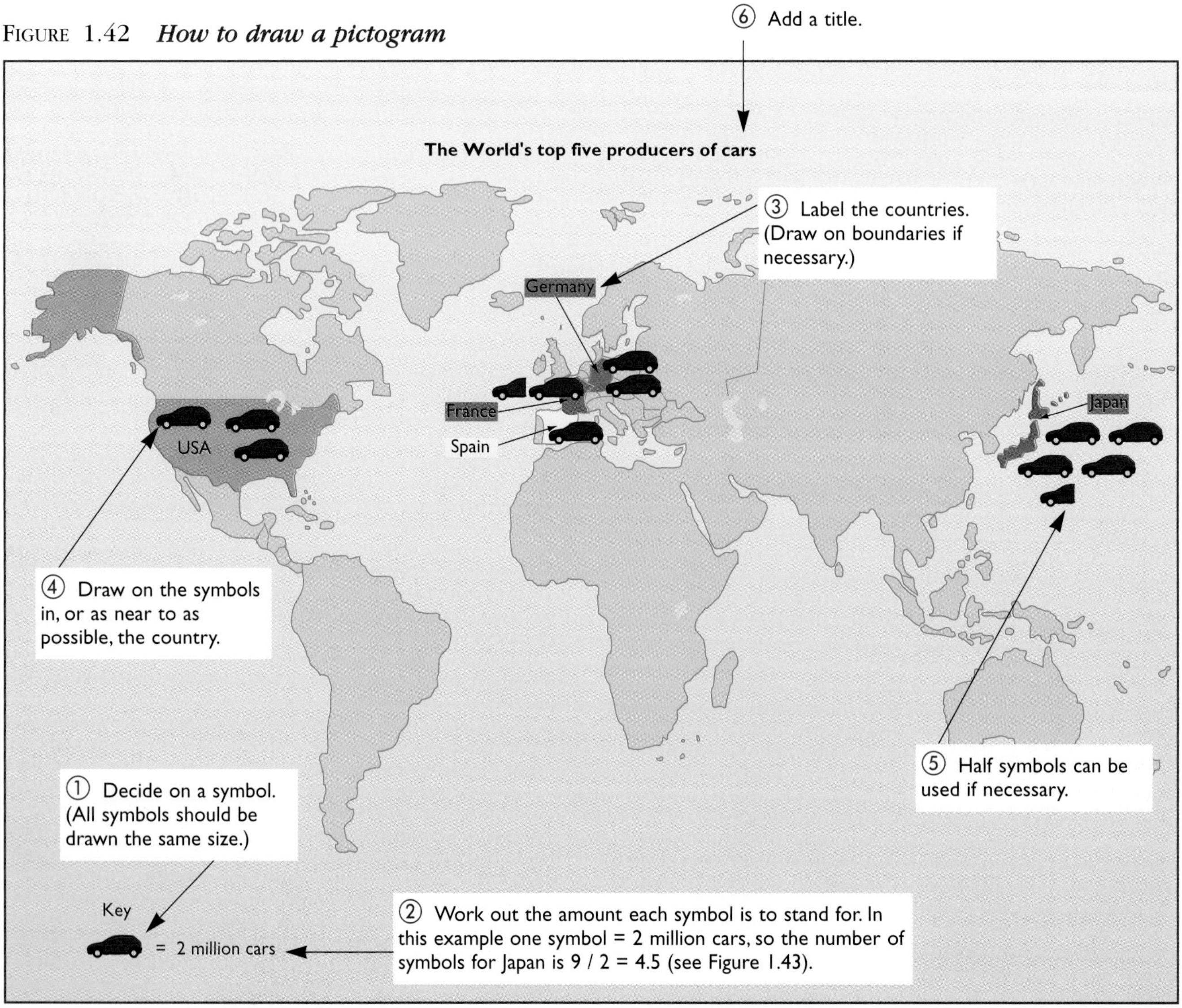

The World's top five producers of cars

⑥ Add a title.

③ Label the countries. (Draw on boundaries if necessary.)

Germany

Japan

France

Spain

USA

④ Draw on the symbols in, or as near to as possible, the country.

⑤ Half symbols can be used if necessary.

① Decide on a symbol. (All symbols should be drawn the same size.)

Key

= 2 million cars

② Work out the amount each symbol is to stand for. In this example one symbol = 2 million cars, so the number of symbols for Japan is 9 / 2 = 4.5 (see Figure 1.43).

W O R K S H O P

1 Complete a copy of Figure 1.44. Do this by working out the number of symbols needed for each country by dividing the production figure by 0.5 (one symbol = 0.5 million tons).
2 Decide on a symbol for ship production. Add it to the key on a copy of Figure 1.42. (Copy only the countries and symbols, not the instructions.)
3 Mark on the number of symbols for each of the five countries in Figure 1.44. (Draw on the boundaries of the country and label it if this has not already been done.)
4 Complete a copy of Figure 1.45. This time you have to decide yourself on what each symbol is going to represent.
5 Decide on a symbol for TV production. Add it to the key on your map.
6 Mark on the number of symbols for each of the five countries in Figure 1.45. (Draw on the boundaries of the country and label it if this has not already been done.)
7 Is there any sort of a pattern on your map? If 'yes', what is it? Can you think of any possible explanations?
8 Does anything shown on your map surprise you? If 'yes', say why? Can you think of anything that might explain your surprising results?

FIGURE 1.43 *The world's top five producers of cars, 1993*

COUNTRY	PRODUCTION (MILLIONS)	NUMBER OF SYMBOLS
JAPAN	9	4.5
USA	6	3
GERMANY	4	2
FRANCE	3	1.5
SPAIN	2	1

FIGURE 1.44 *The world's top five producers of ships, 1994*

COUNTRY	PRODUCTION (MILLION TONS)	NUMBER OF SYMBOLS
JAPAN	8	
SOUTH KOREA	4	
TAIWAN	1	
GERMANY	1	
POLAND	0.5	

(One symbol = 0.5 million tons)

FIGURE 1.45 *The world's top five producers of TV, 1992*

COUNTRY	PRODUCTION (MILLIONS)	NUMBER OF SYMBOLS
CHINA	29	
SOUTH KOREA	16	
USA	14	
JAPAN	12	
AZERBAIJAN	6	

W O R D   B O X

symbol   a small drawing or letter used to represent (show) something

Population pyramids

Introduction

A population pyramid is a type of bar graph that allows you to compare the number or percentage in different age groups and the balance between males and females.

For example, Figure 1.46 shows that India has a much larger percentage of young people than old people. This is because it has a much higher **birth rate** than **death rate**. It also shows that there is a slightly greater percentage of elderly women than men. This is because women, in most countries, tend to live longer than men, for reasons that no one is quite sure of.

You can also get an idea of the balance between the **working** and the **dependent** populations of a place. For example, you can see that India's working population has to support a large dependent population of young people.

FIGURE 1.46 *How to draw a population pyramid*

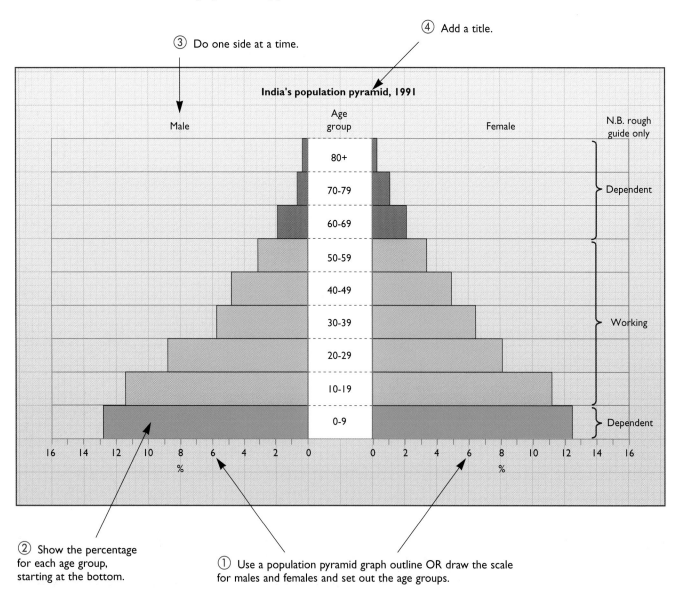

③ Do one side at a time.

④ Add a title.

India's population pyramid, 1991

Male | Age group | Female | N.B. rough guide only

80+
70-79   } Dependent
60-69
50-59
40-49
30-39   } Working
20-29
10-19
0-9   } Dependent

16 14 12 10 8 6 4 2 0   0 2 4 6 8 10 12 14 16
%   %

② Show the percentage for each age group, starting at the bottom.

① Use a population pyramid graph outline OR draw the scale for males and females and set out the age groups.

W O R K S H O P

1 (You will need a copy of Figure 1.47, the population pyramid graph outline, for this activity.) Plot the statistics in Figure 1.48 to show the population structure of the USA.
2 What does your graph tell you about: (a) the USA's birth rate and death rate; (b) the balance between males and females; and (c) its working and dependent populations?

3 Plot the statistics in Figure 1.49 to show the population structure of Thailand.
4 What does your graph tell you about: (a) Thailand's birth rate and death rate; (b) the balance between males and females; and (c) its working and dependent populations?
5 Compare your two graphs. (a) How are they different? (b) How are they similar? (c) Suggest reasons for these similarities and differences.

FIGURE 1.47 *Population pyramid graph outline*

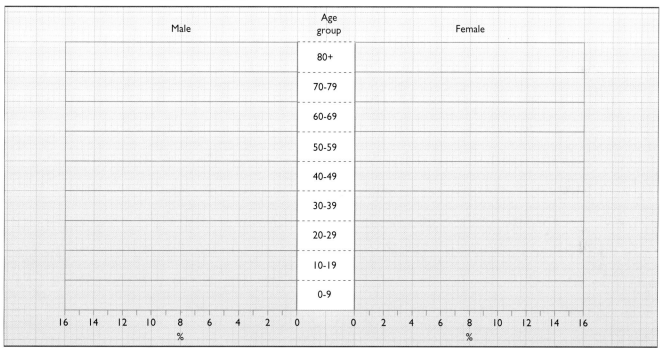

FIGURE 1.48 *Population structure of the USA, 1990*

AGE GROUP	% MALES	% FEMALES
0-9	7.6	7.2
10-19	7.2	6.8
20-29	8.2	8
30-39	8.3	8.5
40-49	6.2	6.4
50-59	4.2	4.5
60-69	3.8	4.5
70-79	2.3	3.3
80+	1	2

FIGURE 1.49 *Population structure of Thailand, 1989*

AGE GROUP	% MALES	% FEMALES
0-9	12	12
10-19	12	12
20-29	9	9
30-39	6.5	6.5
40-49	3.5	4.5
50-59	2.5	3.5
60-69	1.5	2.5
70-79	0.5	1.5
80+	NIL	1

W O R D   B O X

birth rate the number of babies born per 1000 people per year
death rate the number of deaths per 1000 people per year
dependent population those who rely on the working population for support, e.g. the young and elderly
working population people in employment who have to support the dependent population

Triangular graphs

Introduction

A triangular graph is a way of showing three pieces of information that add up to 100 per cent. For example, Figure 1.50 shows the land use of each country divided up into three categories: arable; grass; and 'other' (mainly forest and built-up areas). The percentage for arable is found by reading across (parallel to the solid lines) to the a axis. The percentage for grass is found by reading 'up right' (parallel to the dashed lines) to the b axis. The percentage for 'other' is found by reading 'down right' (parallel to the dotted lines) to the c axis. Figure 1.51 shows how to do this.

The easiest way to plot information on one of these graphs is to mark the figures with a dot on the a, b and c axes and then to join them up with lines parallel to the solid lines for the a axis, dashed lines for the b axis and dotted lines for the c axis.

The Workshop on the next page uses this technique to show the occupational structure of selected countries. Another use would be to show the percentages of sand, clay and silt in a soil.

FIGURE 1.50 *How to read and draw a triangular graph*

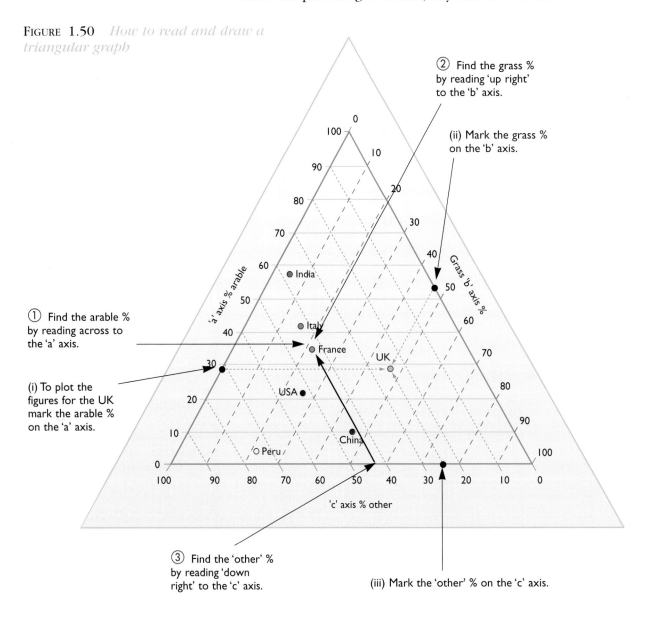

① Find the arable % by reading across to the 'a' axis.

(i) To plot the figures for the UK mark the arable % on the 'a' axis.

② Find the grass % by reading 'up right' to the 'b' axis.

(ii) Mark the grass % on the 'b' axis.

③ Find the 'other' % by reading 'down right' to the 'c' axis.

(iii) Mark the 'other' % on the 'c' axis.

W O R K S H O P

1 Look at Figure 1.50. Write down the land use percentages for each of the following countries: USA, Italy, India, China, Peru.

2 (You will need a copy of the triangular graph outline, Figure 1.52, for this activity.) Plot the statistics in Figure 1.53 as a triangular graph.

3 Write down three differences between the **occupational structures** of the UK and India.

4 Choose one of these differences and try to explain it.

FIGURE 1.51   *Understanding triangular graphs*

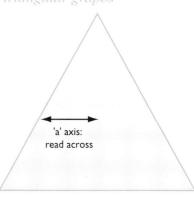

'a' axis: read across

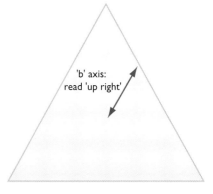

'b' axis: read 'up right'

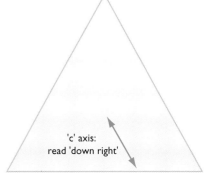

'c' axis: read 'down right'

FIGURE 1.52   *Triangular graph outline*

	% PRIMARY	% SECONDARY	% TERTIARY
MEDCs			
UK	2	20	78
USA	3	18	79
JAPAN	7	24	69
ITALY	9	20	71
FRANCE	7	20	73
LEDCs			
INDIA	62	11	27
BRAZIL	29	16	55
CHINA	73	14	13
PERU	35	12	53
NIGERIA	45	4	51

FIGURE 1.53   *Occupational structure of selected countries*

WORD BOX

arable   land used for growing crops
LEDCs   Less Economically Developed Countries: the poorer countries of mainly South America, Africa and Asia
MEDCs   More Economically Developed Countries: the richer countries of mainly North America and Europe
occupational structure   the balance between primary, secondary and tertiary industry

CHAPTER 2
Atlases and Globes

2.1a Using an atlas

Introduction

An atlas is a book of maps, which contains information such as where physical features like oceans, mountains or rivers are found and the location of countries and cities. The contents page will help you to find a particular map. This will give you a page number to help find a country or continent, or a **thematic** map such as a map showing physical features or climate. Figure 2.2 shows a typical contents page.

Using the index

The **index** is more specific and will help you find a particular place. The index is usually found at the back of the atlas. Despite differences between atlases, the index entries are usually arranged in a similar way:

- Each place is listed in an alphabetical order.
- The index entry for a place will give the place name, its country, a page number and a letter/number reference or latitude/longitude to locate the place on the map.
- Often abbreviations are used to identify specific features, i.e. if a place is a physical feature e.g. The Rhine or The Gulf of Lyon, the actual name is given first in the index: Rhine, River or Lyon, Gulf of (Figure 2.1).
- Where there is more than one place with the same name but in different countries, the name is followed by the country or region. Sheffield, for example:
  Sheffield, England
  Sheffield, New Zealand.
- If the same name is in the same country, then a county or region name is used to order places, for example:
  Avon, R., Bristol,
  Avon, R., Dorset.

FIGURE 2.1 *Some abbreviations used in an atlas index*

Countries

Afghan	Afghanistan
Bangl.	Bangladesh
Dom Rep	Dominican Republic
Lux	Luxembourg
Neth	Netherlands
P.N.G.	Papua New Guinea
R.S.A.	Republic of South Africa
Russ Fed	Russian Federation
Switz.	Switzerland
U.K.	United Kingdom
U.S.A.	United States of America

Physical features

b, B,	bay
des	desert
i, is I	island
l, L	lake
Mt	mountain
Mts	mountains
Oc	ocean
pen, Pen	Peninsula
str, Str	Strait

FIGURE 2.2 *Extract from an atlas index*

PLACENAME/FEATURE	COUNTRY	PAGE NUMBER	MAP REFERENCE	LATITUDE/LONGITUDE
Oriental mts	Peru/Bolivia	76	C3	5N 70W
Orinoco R	Venezuela	74	C7	14S 61W
Orissa	India	97	G5	20N 84E
Oristano	Italy	34	H6	39N 8E
Oristano, Gulf of	Italy	34	H6	39N 8E
Orivesi L	Finland	24	B3	62N 29E

● Some features, such as mountains or seas, cover more than one grid square. The index will give the grid reference where the name is printed (Figure 2.3).

FIGURE 2.3 *Locating physical features*

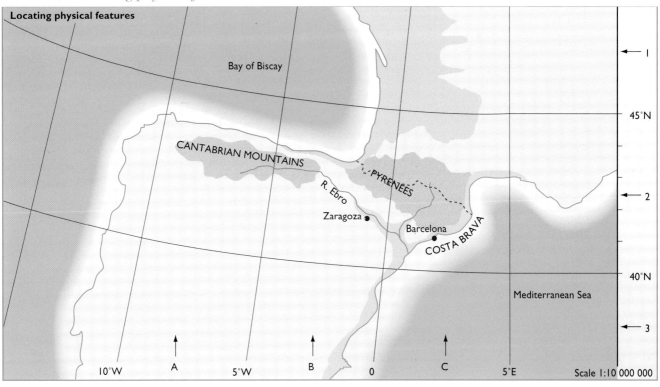

Locating physical features

W O R K S H O P

You will need an atlas to help with these questions.

1 Copy and complete this paragraph using the contents page of your atlas.

The contents page is found at the _____ of the atlas. After looking at the contents pages, I found a map of the British Isles on page _____, a map of Australia on page _____ and a map of the world on page _____. The index starts on page _____ of the atlas.

2 Using the contents page, how many different types of map are listed? Give three examples. Find these in the atlas and write a sentence to describe each.

3 From the index, find how many places are called London. Write down where each is found.
Can you find three other examples of places with the same name?

4 Use the contents page and index to find out whether these places are either a city, a sea, an island, a country, or a mountain range, and say where they can be found.
Manila Majorca Costa Rica Galapagos Tashkent
Ob Adriatic Orkney Comoros Nairobi
Andes Hwang-Ho Mekong Tibet Taiwan
Pyrennes Okhotsk Great Divide Latvia Ural

index an alphabetical list
location where a place is found
thematic map a map that shows one particular feature of the geography of an area

2.1b Letter co-ordinates

Introduction

We use maps to locate places and features such as cities, mountains and rivers. To help locate places a **map grid** system is used. Each grid square is identified using the letters and numbers along the top and side of the map.

Using letter/number co-ordinates

To locate a grid square you first read across the top to find the letter, then up the side to find the number (Figure 2.4). Where they cross gives the map co-ordinate. Figure 2.5 shows part of the Sheffield street map. In U29 is The University of Sheffield and in W31 are The Law Courts.

FIGURE 2.4 *Using letter co-ordinates. Read across first, letter B, then up to find the number 4. At B4 there is a hotel*

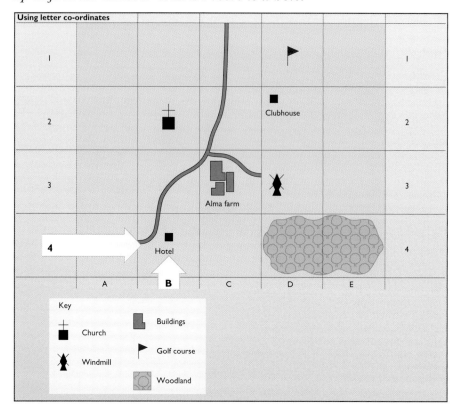

FIGURE 2.5 *Extract from Sheffield map*

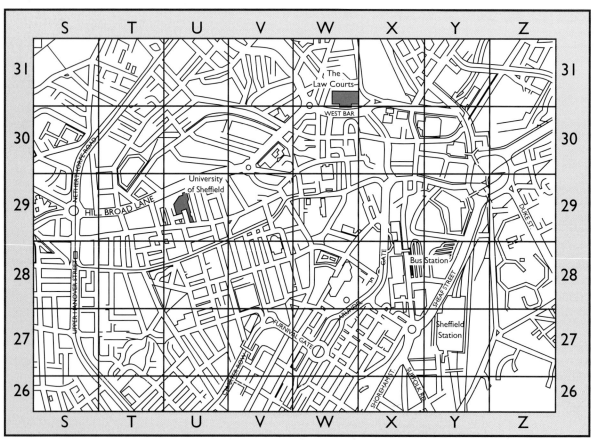

Figure 2.6 shows an atlas map of Europe. Because the earth is curved, the lines do not form squares.

1 Which city is found in each of these grid co-ordinates:
F4 G6 K4 C7 I4 G5?
2 Give the grid co-ordinates for each of these cities:
London Paris Moscow Rome Sofia Lisbon?
3 In which squares are these countries
France Finland Romania Netherlands?
4 In which square would you find:
The Sea of Azov Sicily?

W O R D   B O X

map co-ordinates   a way of identifying a square
map grid   a system of lines that run north–south and east–west across the map to form a grid

FIGURE 2.6   *Atlas map of Europe*

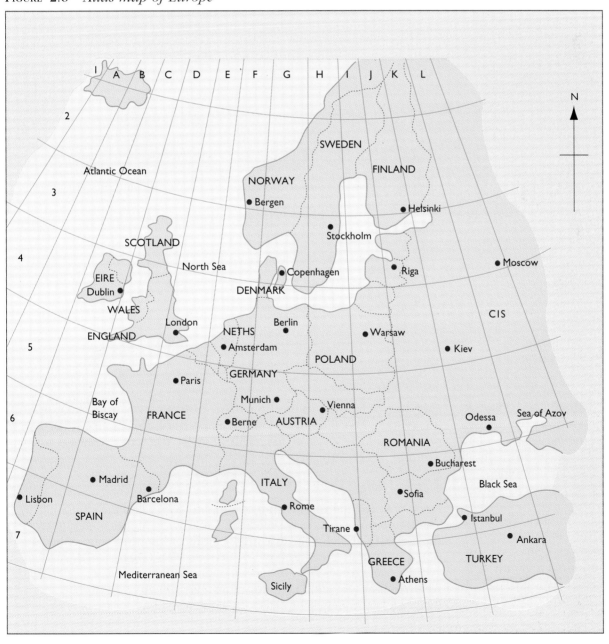

2.1c Latitude and longitude

Introduction

Lines of latitude and longitude are drawn on world maps to form a grid for locating places. Lines of latitude run east to west and go around the earth. The 0 line of latitude is called the equator. Lines of latitude are parallel circles and number either north or south of the equator. Figure 2.7 shows the important lines of latitude and longitude.

FIGURE 2.7 *World map showing important lines of longitude and latitude*

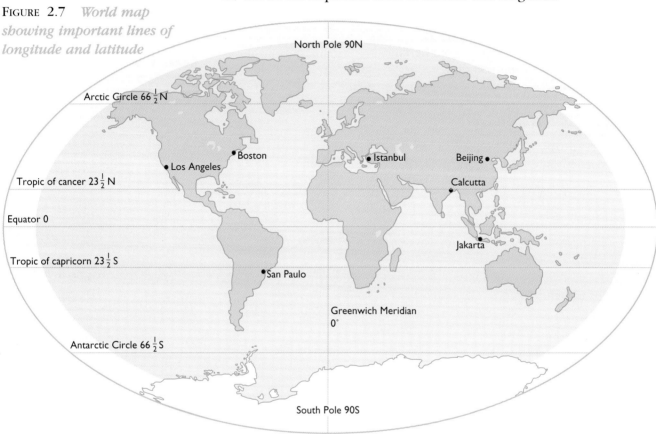

Latitude

Each line of latitude shows how many degrees away from the **equator** it is (Figure 2.8). If a line of latitude is north of the equator it has a number and the letter 'N' for north, likewise the letter 'S' means it is south of the equator.

Longitude

Lines of longitude run north to south and go up and down the earth. The 0 line of longitude is called the Greenwich Meridian and goes through Greenwich Park in London. Lines of longitude curve into the poles and number east and west of Greenwich (Figure 2.8).

Each place has its own latitude and longitude co-ordinate. For example, New York is 41N 74W. The index of an atlas will give the latitude and longitude co-ordinates for places. By finding where the line latitude 41N meets line longitude 74W New York's position can be plotted.

WORD BOX

equator the 0 degree line of latitude around the middle of the earth
Greenwich Meridian the 0 degree line of longitude which passes through London
latitude grid lines which run east to west
longitude grid lines which run north to south
millionaire city a city with a population of over one million people

W O R K S H O P

1 Use an atlas to complete the missing co-ordinates in Figure 2.9.
2 Some of the cities listed in Figure 2.9 have been plotted on Figure 2.7.
   a) Plot the millionaire cities on a copy of a world map.
   b) Using an atlas, find and plot other millionaire cities.
3 Most of the world's largest cities are found between the Tropic of Cancer and Capricorn.
   a) On your world map, draw and label these two lines of latitude.
   b) Describe the distribution of cities.
   c) Suggest three reasons why some areas have no or few millionaire cities.

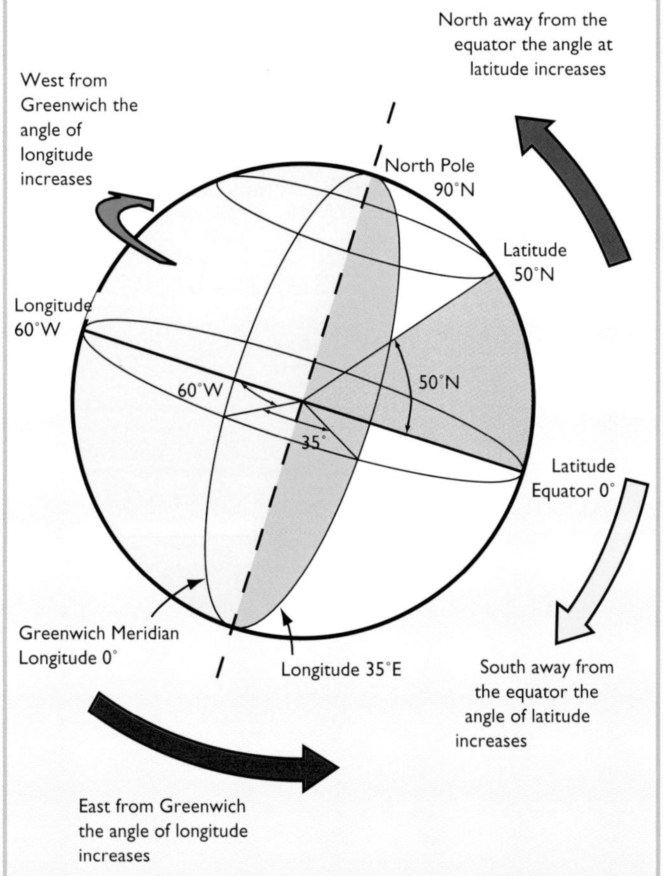

CITY	LATITUDE (nearest degree)	LONGITUDE (nearest degree)
Bangkok	14N	E
Beijing	39N	116E
Bombay	19N	E
Boston	N	71W
Buenos Aires	35S	58W
Cairo	30N	31E
Calcutta	23N	E
Chicago	N	88W
Delhi	29N	77E
Istanbul	41N	29E
Jakarta	6S	W
Karachi	25N	67E
Lima	12S	77W
London	52N	?
Los Angeles	34N	118W
Madras	13N	W
Manila	15N	121W
Mexico City	N	99W
New York	41N	74W
Rio de Janeiro	23S	43W
Santiago	S	71W
Sao Paulo	24S	47W
Seoul	38N	127W
Sydney	S	151W
Tokyo	36N	140W

FIGURE 2.8 *Finding latitude and longitude*

Finding the angle of latitude and longitude

FIGURE 2.9 *Co-ordinates of selected millionaire cities*

2.2a *Thematic maps*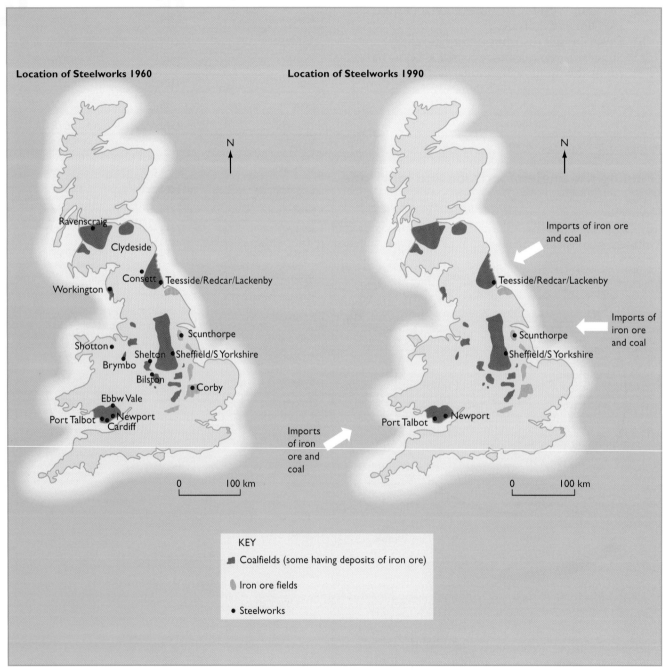

Introduction

Maps that show one particular feature of the geography of an area are called **thematic maps**. They can be used to show the **distribution** of features, e.g. farms, industry or mines. Figure 2.10 shows the UK iron and steel production. In some areas the manufacturing centres are clustered together. Figure 2.10 shows how the distribution has changed.

FIGURE 2.10 *Location of steelworks, 1960 and 1990*

FIGURE 2.11 *World gold producing companies*

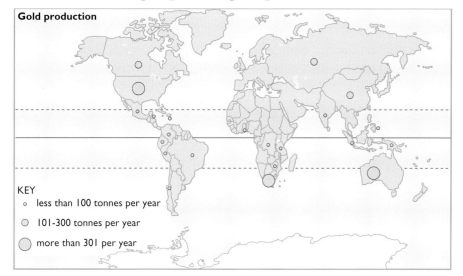

Gold production

KEY
○ less than 100 tonnes per year
◎ 101-300 tonnes per year
◉ more than 301 per year

Plotting maps

A **symbol** has been used in Figure 2.11 to show producers of gold. A thematic map can be used to show how much a country is producing. **Proportional symbols** can be drawn to represent the amount produced. Figure 2.11 is a proportional symbol map which shows the distribution of gold producers and importance of each country.

W O R K S H O P

1 Copy and complete the paragraph using Figure 2.10.
   In 1960 there were _____ major steelworks. Most of these steelworks were located on either a coalfield with some on the _____ or _____. South Wales was an important steel making region with works at _____, _____, _____ and _____. There were few steelworks built on the coast, most were located _____.
   By 1990, there were only _____ steelworks. There has been a _____ in the number of steelworks. There are two main areas for steel production in South Wales at _____ and _____, Sheffield and Scunthorpe, and at _____. Two major areas are located on the coast. Here they are supplied with _____ of iron ore and coal.
Words to use: *inland, fifteen, five, coast, iron ore fields, decline, imports, Teesside, Port Talbot, Newport, Ebbw Vale, Cardiff.*

2 Using an atlas, study Figure 2.11:
   a) Which countries are the largest producers of gold?
   b) How many countries are gold producers?
3 Using Figure 2.12:
   a) Plot on a world map outline the iron ore producers as proportional symbols.
   b) Write a paragraph to describe the distribution of iron ore producers.

FIGURE 2.12 *World iron ore producers, million tonnes*

1	China	235
2	Brazil	152
3	Australia	116
4	Ukraine	75
5	India	56
6	USA	55
7	Russia	40
8	Canada	34
9	S Africa	30
10	Sweden	19
11	Kazakhstan	18
12	Venezuela	17
13	N Korea	10
14	Iran	10
15	Mauritania	9
16	Chile	8

W O R D   B O X

distribution   where something is found
proportional symbol   a sign drawn to a scale to show an amount
symbol   a small drawing or letter used to represent (show) something
thematic map   a map that shows one particular aspect of the geography of an area

2.2b World ecosystems

Introduction

Atlases contain many examples of thematic maps, one is natural vegetation. Figure 2.13 shows a generalized **ecosystem** map. This shows three broad types of natural vegetation: forest, grassland and desert, but many more specialist groups exist within these groups. These represent areas of natural vegetation before people began to farm and shape the landscape to meet their needs. Each ecosystem produces different amounts of natural vegetation. This is known as its **primary production**.

FIGURE 2.13 *Generalised world ecosystems*

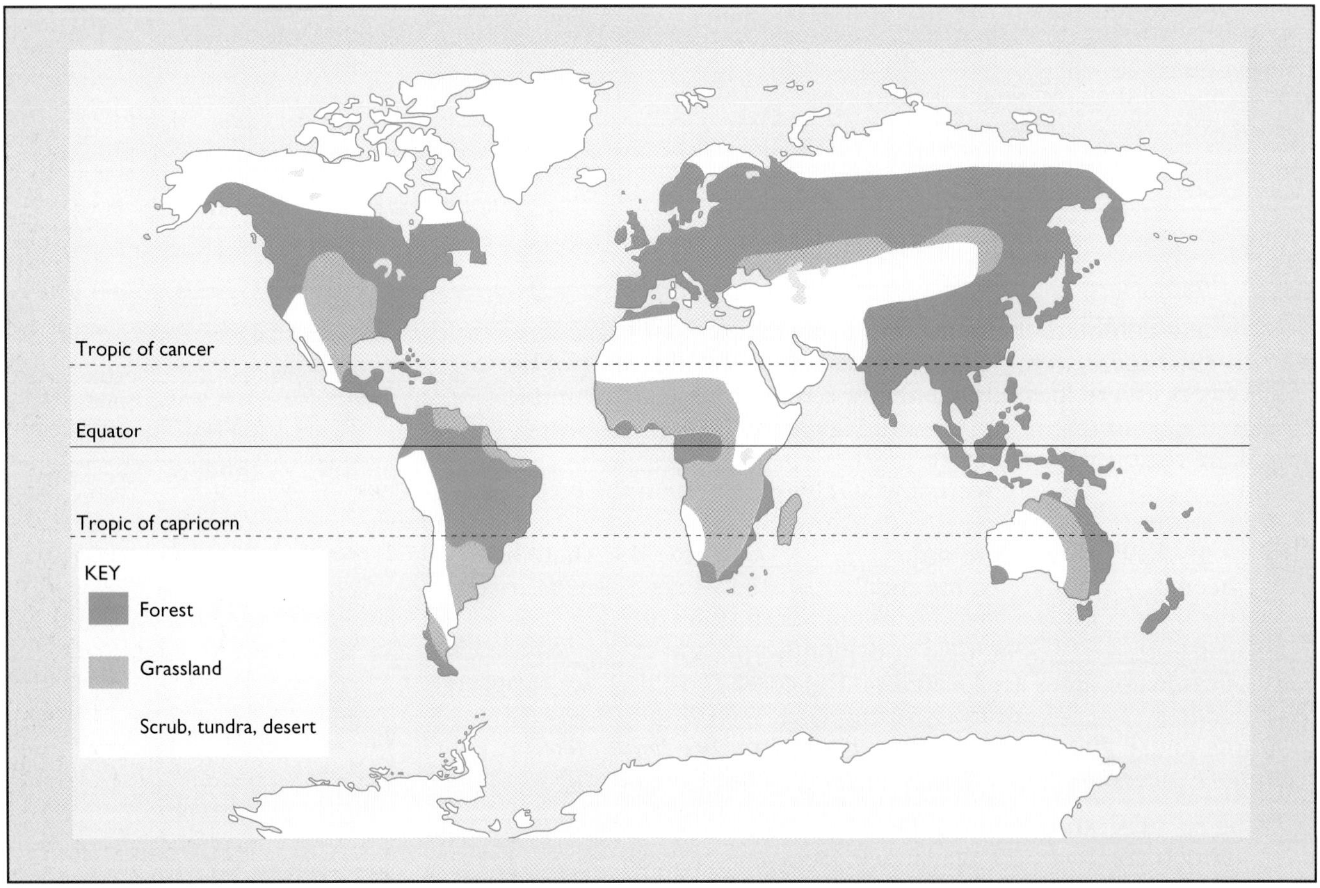

Tropic of cancer

Equator

Tropic of capricorn

KEY

Forest

Grassland

Scrub, tundra, desert

Using thematic maps

By using a range of thematic maps about a topic, it is possible to interpret reasons for a distribution. Water and temperature together are two important factors and these vary considerably across the world (Figures 2.14 and 2.15).

The average temperature decreases as you move north or south away from the equator. Grass growth stops when temperatures fall below 6°C. In the colder Antarctic and Arctic regions there is little growth. In the temperate regions there is seasonal growth, but in the tropics plants grow all year.

The lack of water in areas like hot deserts such as the Sahara or Gobi Deserts reduces plant growth. Where reliable rainfall occurs, as in equatorial or temperate regions, there is lush growth.

FIGURE 2.14 *World water budget*

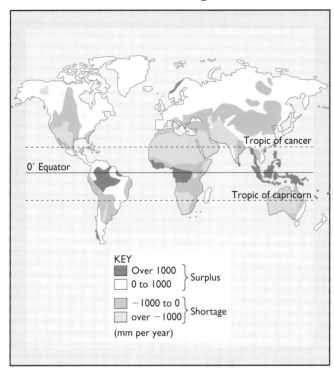

KEY
■ Over 1000 } Surplus
□ 0 to 1000 }
▨ −1000 to 0 } Shortage
▨ over −1000 }
(mm per year)

FIGURE 2.15 *World temperature*

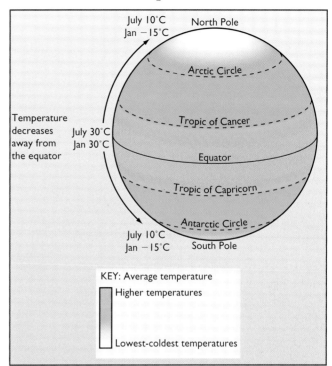

KEY: Average temperature
▨ Higher temperatures
□ Lowest-coldest temperatures

W O R K S H O P

1 Using the data in Figure 2.16, plot on an outline map of Figure 2.13 the percentage of world biomass data. Devise a key to show high and low producers.
2 Describe the **biomass** pattern shown on your map.
3 Using the data in Figure 2.16, plot on an outline map of Figure 2.13 the approximate dry production. Devise a key to show high, moderate and low producers.
4 Describe the pattern of dry production shown on your map.
5 What factors have influenced the amount of primary production shown on your maps?

W O R D   B O X

biomass the amount of animals and plants
ecosystem consists of all the plants and animals, and other things such as soil and water, which make up a natural region
primary production the amount of vegetation produced by an ecosystem

FIGURE 2.16 *Generalised world primary production*

ECOSYSTEM	APPROXIMATE DRY PRODUCTION (grams per square metre per year)	PERCENTAGE OF THE WORLD BIOMASS
Tropical forest	2 000	50
Temperate forest	1 100	44
Savanna grasslands	700	3
Tundra and ice caps	140	2
Deserts	71	1

2.2c Plotting development indicators

Introduction

Maps provide a useful resource with which to compare patterns of economic and social development. Figure 2.17 shows that there is an uneven spread of wealth (**Gross National Product per person**). The map shows that the poorer nations, (Less Economically Developed Countries, or LEDCs), are located in the south and the richer nations, More Economically Developed Countries, or MEDCs), are in the north. The pattern shown can be simplified by drawing on a north–south divide.

Plotting development data

Using a single indicator to describe levels of development does not give a full picture. It is better to use a broader range of **indicators**. Development includes economic, social, population and standard of living indicators. These could be plotted singly, e.g. Figure 2.17, or as a base map with overlays – each with a different indicator. (See 'How to draw graded maps', pages 94–95).

Another technique involves calculating and plotting an index, e.g. Physical Quality of Life Index (**PQLI**), which uses several indicators (Figure 2.18). This index uses **life expectancy**, **infant mortality** and **adult literacy**. Each country is then scaled: 0—the worst; 100—the best. Each country then has its three scalings averaged to give its PQLI. A PQLI of 90 indicates a high level of well-being and below 77 indicates less than a minimum level of well-being. Computer generated maps provide a powerful tool in investigating issues such as development and links between various indicators (see pages 146–147). The skill is how these maps are interpreted and in the choice of appropriate data to plot.

(See 'How to draw graded maps', pages 94–95). ... (see pages 146–147).

WORD BOX

adult literacy percentage of a country's population over 15 with basic literacy skills

gross national product per person GNP/capita, a measure of wealth per person in a country; calculated by dividing the total value of all goods and services produced in a country by its population

indicator statistics that tell us something about a place, e.g. how economically developed it is

infant mortality number of babies who die before they are one year old, for every 1000 babies that are born

life expectancy average lifespan of a person

PQLI a composite figure derived from data analysis, which measures levels of development

FIGURE 2.17 *World Gross National Product*

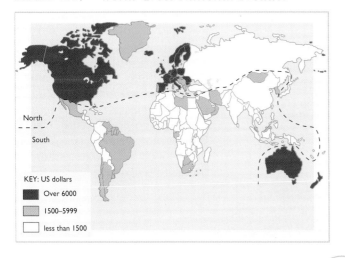

KEY: US dollars
- Over 6000
- 1500–5999
- less than 1500

FIGURE 2.18 *People Quality of Life Index (PQLI) Map*

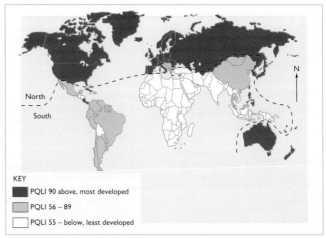

KEY
- PQLI 90 above, most developed
- PQLI 56 – 89
- PQLI 55 – below, least developed

WORKSHOP

1 Using Figure 2.17:
 a) Which continents have the richest countries? Name two examples.
 b) Which continents have the poorest countries? Name two examples.

2 Suggest two drawbacks in using a single indicator to describe levels of development.
3 Using Figure 2.18:
 a) Describe the pattern of development shown.
 b) Are there any similarities with Figure 2.17?

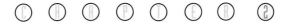

4 The data in Figure 2.20 can be used to compare levels of development in North and South America.
  a) Devise a method to show the level of development for each country.
  b) Plot this on an outline map of North and South America.
  c) Describe and compare the pattern of development.

5 Compare your maps with Figure 2.19. Describe any similarities between the maps.

6 The data in Figure 2.20 can be used to produce an index to devise your own method.
  a) Calculate an index for each country.
  b) Plot the index on an outline map of North and South America.
  c) Describe the pattern of development shown.

7 Compare your three methods of presenting data. Which map gives the most accurate representation of levels of development? Explain reasons for your choice.

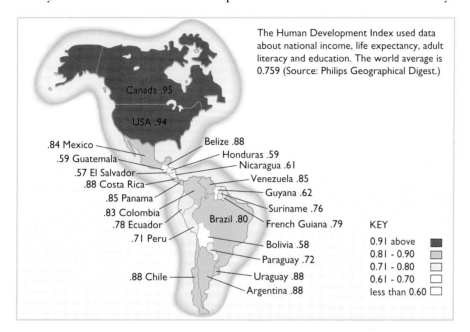

The Human Development Index used data about national income, life expectancy, adult literacy and education. The world average is 0.759 (Source: Philips Geographical Digest.)

Canada .95
USA .94
.84 Mexico
.59 Guatemala
.57 El Salvador
.88 Costa Rica
.85 Panama
.83 Colombia
.78 Ecuador
.71 Peru
.88 Chile
Belize .88
Honduras .59
Nicaragua .61
Venezuela .85
Guyana .62
Suriname .76
Brazil .80
French Guiana .79
Bolivia .58
Paraguay .72
Uraguay .88
Argentina .88

KEY
0.91 above
0.81 - 0.90
0.71 - 0.80
0.61 - 0.70
less than 0.60

FIGURE 2.19 *Human Development Index. This is based on income, life expectancy, adult literacy and education data*

FIGURE 2.20 *Economic and Social Indicators for the Americas*

Country	Life exp. years		% Employment Agr. Services		Average income $ per person	Roads per km /1 000km2	Pop. / doctor	% Adult literacy	Trade per person
	M	F	M	F					
Argentina	68	75	13%	53%	$7 290	21 km	329	96%	$877
Belize	67	72	18%	10%	$2 440	22 km	1 500	96%	$1 967
Bolivia	54	58	47%	34%	$650	2 km	1 500	78%	$237
Brazil	64	69	25%	50%	$2 920	20 km	1 000	81%	$343
Canada	74	81	5%	72%	$21 206	31 km	450	99%	$9 355
Chile	69	76	19%	55%	$2 160	15 km	2 150	93%	$1 221
Colombia	66	72	2%	77%	$1 280	10 km	1 000	87%	$364
Costa Rica	52	57	25%	48%	$1 930	104 km	1 030	93%	$1 110
Ecuador	65	69	33%	48%	$1 170	13 km	671	88%	$498
El Salvador	64	69	11%	66%	$1 320	72 km	1 563	70%	$481
French Guinea	69	76	9%	76%	$5 000	6 km	700	82%	$4 762
Guatemala	62	67	50%	32%	$1 110	27 km	4 000	54%	$399
Guyana	62	68	27%	47%	$350	3 km	6 000	98%	$833
Honduras	64	68	38%	47%	$580	15 km	1 266	71%	$348
Mexico	67	74	23%	48%	$3 750	43 km	621	87%	$1 507
Nicaragua	65	68	46%	38%	$360	34 km	2 000	65%	$269
Panama	71	75	27%	59%	$2 580	37 km	562	90%	$1 049
Paraguay	65	70	48%	31%	$1 500	7 km	1 587	91%	$461
Peru	63	67	35%	55%	$1 490	6 km	1 031	87%	$369
Surinam	68	73	20%	60%	$1 210	3 km	1 200	92%	$2 360
USA	73	80	3%	69%	$24 750	380 km	420	99%	$4 611
Uruguay	69	76	5%	73%	$3 190	38 km	500	96%	$1 260

2.3a *Mercator versus Peters*

Introduction

One of the most difficult problems a **cartographer** has is producing a flat map of the earth. Atlas maps are shown as a flat surface, but the earth is a **sphere** (Figure 2.21).

FIGURE 2.21 *Earth from space*

Cylindrical projections

Cartographers use a system of projections to draw flat maps of the earth. To do this, changes are made to the size and shape of the oceans and continents. The choice of **projection** depends on the purpose of the map. But whatever projection is used the map is likely to be distorted. Figure 2.22 shows the cylindrical projection that is commonly used in atlases. There are three common forms: Mercator; Peter's; and Eckert. Each provide a projection showing the continents and oceans. Antarctica is not shown fully.

FIGURE 2.22 *Cylindrical projection*

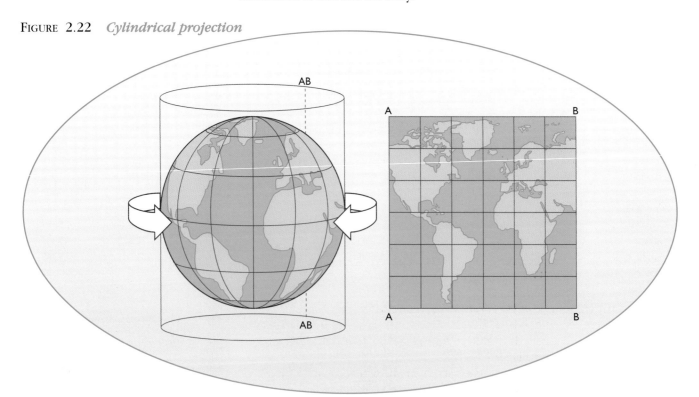

The Mercator projection has the disadvantage of magnifying the size of continents as you go away from the equator. It also promotes a **Eurocentric** view of the world, making Europe more important because of its position and size. The Peter's projection is an equal area map but the shape and distances are badly distorted, i.e. Africa appears twice as long as wide, when in reality it is as wide as it is long. Finally, the Eckert IV is also an equal area map but does not distort the shape of the continents so badly (Figure 2.23).

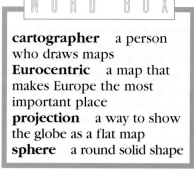

WORD BOX

cartographer a person who draws maps
Eurocentric a map that makes Europe the most important place
projection a way to show the globe as a flat map
sphere a round solid shape

FIGURE 2.23 *Three different world maps drawn using a cylindrical projection*

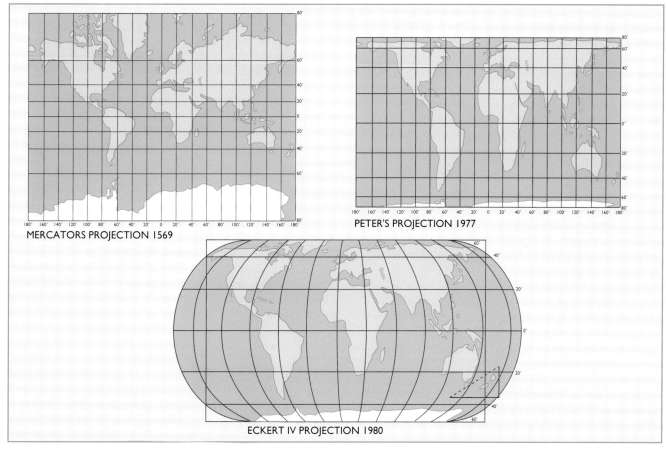

MERCATORS PROJECTION 1569

PETER'S PROJECTION 1977

ECKERT IV PROJECTION 1980

W O R K S H O P

1 Look at Figure 2.23. This shows three world projections.
   a) Draw or trace Africa for each projection.
   b) Say how each projection shows Africa.
   c) Which do you think is the best shape for Africa?
2 To test the problem, a cartographer has in producing a flat map of the world, take a piece of paper 20.5 cm 3 10 cm, cut and shape the paper to fit a tennis ball. Use the Gore projection in the Resource Pack to cover the tennis ball.
3 What other solid shapes could be used to show a flat world map? Try making a cube- or dodecahedron-shaped world!

2.3b Great arcs

Introduction

From space it is easy to see that the earth is a sphere. People who fly notice that the horizon is curved. Ships that sail away seem to sink slowly beneath the water level. This is evidence that the earth is curved.

Great circles

A **great circle** is the largest circle that can be drawn on a globe. The centre of a great circle passes through the centre of the earth. A great arc is part of a great circle and is the shortest distance between any two points on the earth's surface.

FIGURE 2.24 *Great Arcs*

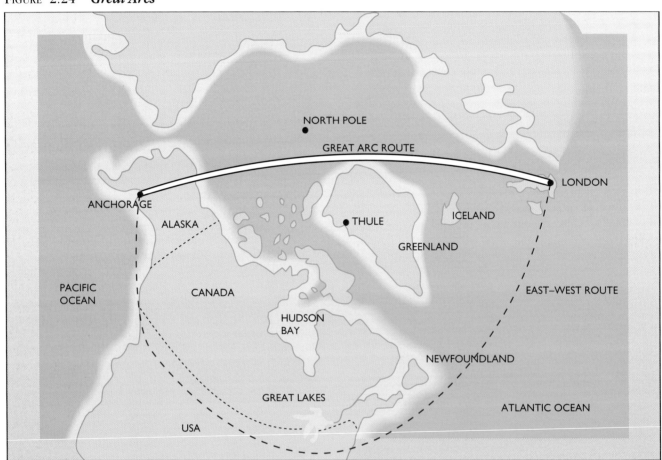

Great arcs

Great arcs are important for navigators who want to find the shortest distance between two points on a great circle. Navigators use special maps that have been specially drawn to show great arcs as straight lines, e.g. Mexico City and Nagpur in India are two places on a great circle, longitude 100 west and 80 east. They both lie on the same line of latitude, 20 north. The great arc distance over the pole is shorter than the east-west distance along the line of latitude (Figure 2.24). Great arc courses can be found using a small globe and piece of string (Figure 2.25). The string is held and stretched between the two places on the globe. An elastic band can be used to show the great circle by placing it around the globe.

1 Use a globe to compare the great arc and east-west routes between the following places: Bangkok and Panama; Los Angeles and Mashhad (Iran); New York and Beijing.

2 Figure 2.24 shows a British Airways route map between London and Anchorage. The aircraft left Heathrow at 1 pm and arrived in Anchorage at 11 pm. The aircraft travelled at an average of 800 km per hour.

  a) Describe the route taken by the aircraft.

  b) Work out the time taken.

  c) Work out the flight distance covered by the aircraft flying over the North Pole.

  d) Use the globe to work out the east-west distance. Which is the shortest route?

3 Using a globe work out and describe the shortest route (the great arc) between these places:

London and Tokyo   London and Sydney
London and Delhi   London and Vancouver
London and Mexico City London and Sao Paolo

great arc part of a great arc circle
great circle the largest circle that can be drawn on a globe

FIGURE 2.25 *A Great Arc shown on a globe using an elastic band*

2.3c Comparing map projections

Introduction

There are over 200 different map projections. These can be grouped as four main categories of map projection: azimuthal; conic; cylindrical; and an individual or special projection. Each map projection attempts to show the earth or part of the earth as a flat surface. The choice of projection depends on the purpose of the map. Each main type of projection has several variations.

Azimuthal projections

Azimuthal projections are centred about a point and have a wheel-like symmetry. The projections are drawn by projecting part of a globe on to a plane which touches the globe only at one point. The projection can be polar, equatorial or an **oblique** view (Figure 2.26). This projection can be used to show areas that have similar east–west and north–south distances.

FIGURE 2.26 *Azimuthal projection*

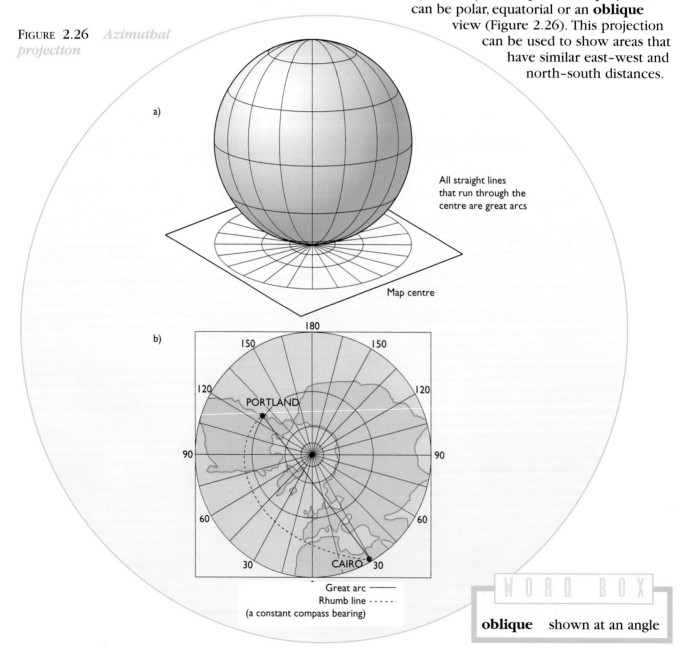

a)

All straight lines that run through the centre are great arcs

Map centre

b)

180

150   150

120   120

PORTLAND

90   90

60   60

30   CAIRO   30

Great arc ———
Rhumb line -----
(a constant compass bearing)

W O R D   B O X

oblique   shown at an angle

Conic projections

Conic projections are drawn by projecting part of the globe on to a cone which just touches a circle on the globe. This is then spread to form a flat map which is part of a circle. The lines of longitude converge to a common point at the poles. The lines of latitude form concentric circles centred on the poles (Figure 2.27). Conic projections can be used to show areas between 30N and 60N, and 30S and 60S, particularly where the east-west is longer than the north-south distance.

FIGURE 2.27 *Conic projection*

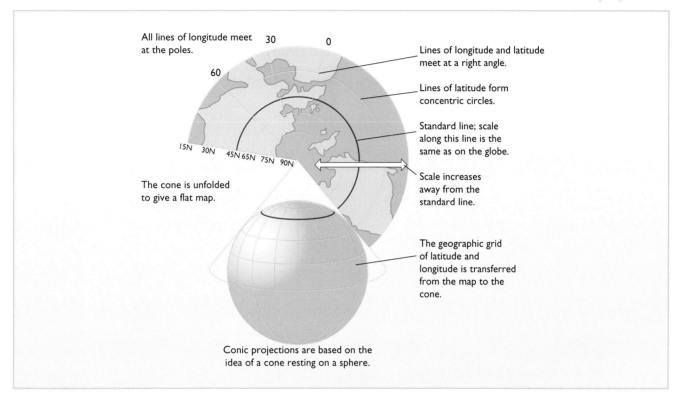

All lines of longitude meet at the poles.

30   0

60

Lines of longitude and latitude meet at a right angle.

Lines of latitude form concentric circles.

Standard line; scale along this line is the same as on the globe.

15N 30N 45N 65N 75N 90N

Scale increases away from the standard line.

The cone is unfolded to give a flat map.

The geographic grid of latitude and longitude is transferred from the map to the cone.

Conic projections are based on the idea of a cone resting on a sphere.

Cylindrical projections

Cylindrical projections are drawn by projecting the surface of the globe on to a cylinder which is just touching the globe. This projection uses horizontal and vertical lines. The finished map is rectangular and the whole globe can be shown as a flat map (see pages 46-47). It is a useful projection for areas between 15N and 15S of the equator. Beyond this there is too much distortion. This projection is useful for plotting routes as straight lines.

W O R K S H O P

1 Using an atlas, find examples of how each type of projection has been used.
2 Use an atlas to find three different projections of Australia.
   a) Trace each projection. Note the projection used.
   b) Which projection gives the best shape of the continent?
   c) Write about the advantages and disadvantages of each projection.

CHAPTER 3

Map reading skills

3.1a *Rivers and symbols*

Introduction

A map uses **symbols** instead of words. Symbols are small drawings which can look like the real thing, e.g. a church with a tower is ✠, or abbreviations, e.g. P for post office. A map has a key that lists what each symbol means.

Using symbols

Symbols can be used to show different types of houses or land use in an area. They can also be used to show physical features, e.g. features along a river (Figure 3.1). This type of map is called a **morphometric map**. Such maps are useful in describing and identifying patterns in the landscape.

FIGURE 3.1   *River features map*

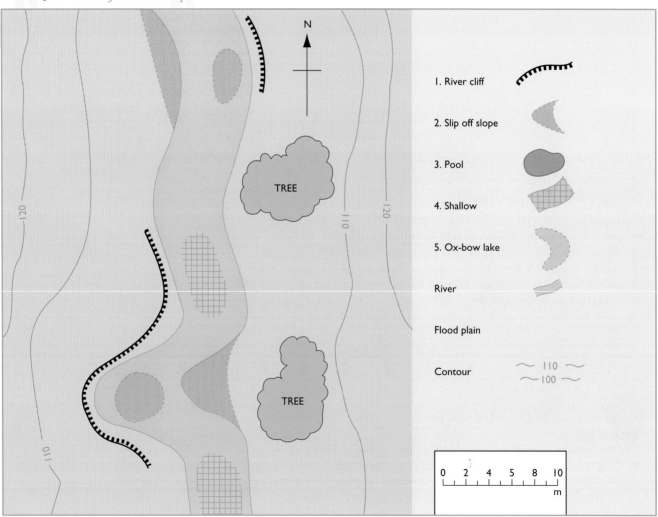

1 Find the key to the 1:50 000 map on page 84. The symbols can be shown as drawings, patches, letters and lines.
   a) Draw and label five symbols that look like pictures.
   b) List five symbols that are letters.
   c) Draw and label three symbols that are patches.
   d) Draw and label three symbols that are lines.

2 Find the water feature symbols. Draw a map that uses at least five of these features.

3 (You will need a copy of the base map Figure 3.2.) Draw on or colour in the symbol that goes with each number. Use the same symbols as in Figure 3.1.

4 Study your completed map. Describe the pattern of river features you would find going down stream.

FIGURE 3.2 *Base map*

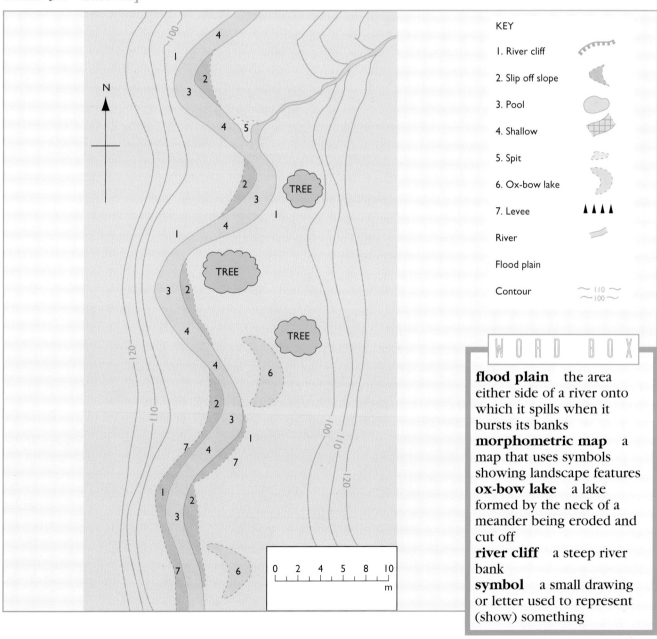

KEY

1. River cliff
2. Slip off slope
3. Pool
4. Shallow
5. Spit
6. Ox-bow lake
7. Levee
River
Flood plain
Contour

WORD BOX

flood plain   the area either side of a river onto which it spills when it bursts its banks
morphometric map   a map that uses symbols showing landscape features
ox-bow lake   a lake formed by the neck of a meander being eroded and cut off
river cliff   a steep river bank
symbol   a small drawing or letter used to represent (show) something

3.1b Rivers and height

Introduction

Maps are drawn on flat sheets of paper, so how are hills and valleys shown? Height can be shown as a spot height, which gives an exact height for a point. However, the landscape is made up of different **natural features**. These features can be shown by joining up places of the same height using **contour** lines.

FIGURE 3.3 *A view of a drainage basin*

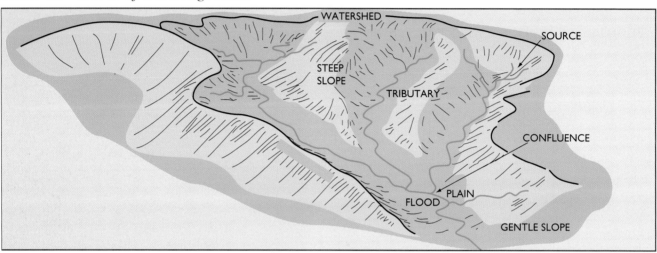

FIGURE 3.4 *Contour map with graded shading*

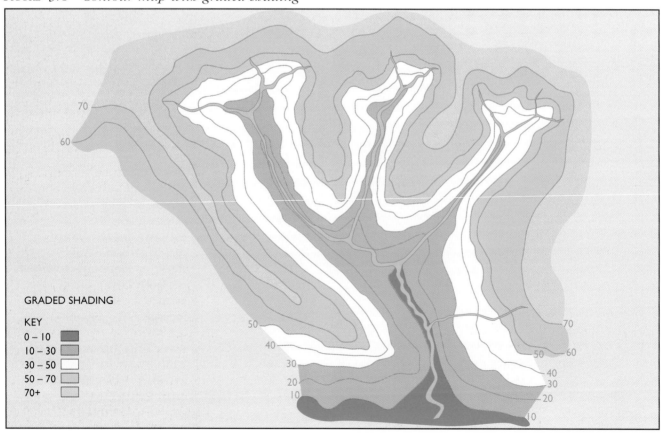

GRADED SHADING

KEY

0 – 10
10 – 30
30 – 50
50 – 70
70+

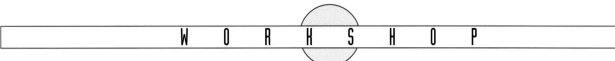

Relief on a map

Figure 3.3 shows a river drainage basin. The same area is shown as a contour map in Figure 3.4. Features in the river landscape can be identified from their contour patterns. Where contour lines are close together this is a steep slope. If the contours are spaced out, there is a gentle slope.

By colouring the areas between the contour lines a graded shading map is produced (see pages 94-95). This makes the areas of low and high land easy to see.

FIGURE 3.5 *Base map*

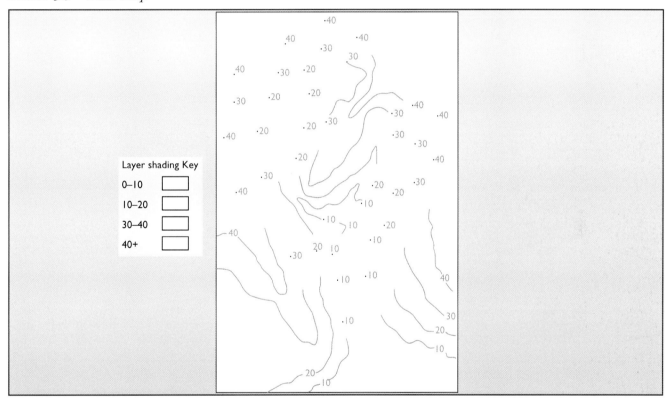

1 a) Use a copy of base map Figure 3.5 to complete the contour map.
   b) Use the key to complete a layer shaded map.
2 On your copy of Figure 3.5, identify and label the following river features: (a) flood plain; (b) tributary valley; (c) **watershed**; (d) steep valley side.
3 Use your completed map to write a paragraph to describe the river landscape.
4 Use the OS map of Bakewell (Extract 3) to:
   a) trace these contours: 125 m, 150 m and 170 m;
   b) draw on the rivers Lathkill and Derwent;
   c) shade in the flood plain green;
   d) complete the layer shading using a different colour for areas between the contours. Add a key and title to your map. Use grid references to accurately locate features;
   e) describe the landscape features shown.

contour a line that joins up points of equal height
natural feature features in the landscape produced by natural processes
drainage basin also called the *catchment area*, is an area of land drained by a river system
watershed a ridge that divides two drainage basins

3.1c Rivers and cross-sections

Introduction

A **cross-section** is a diagram that gives a cut away or side view of the landscape. A series of cross-sections can be used to show how the shape of a river changes downstream from its source. Cross-sections from different parts of the valley can be compared (Figure 3.6).

Long profile

The length and **gradient** of a slope can be shown with a long profile (Figure 3.6). The profile is drawn along the length of the river. A piece of paper is placed along the course of the river. Contours are marked where they cross the river. These marks are transferred onto a chart and joined to give a smooth line. This is the **long profile**.

FIGURE 3.6 *Valley cross-section and long profile*

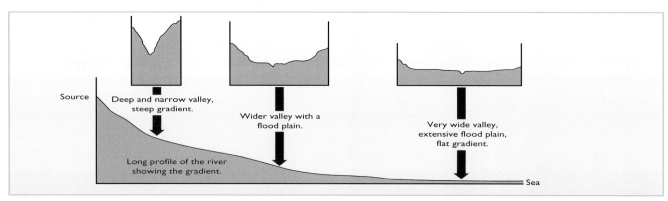

FIGURE 3.7 *Base map*

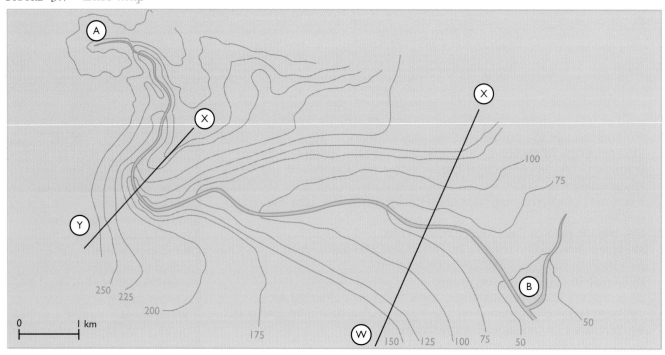

Figure 3.8 *How to draw a cross-section*

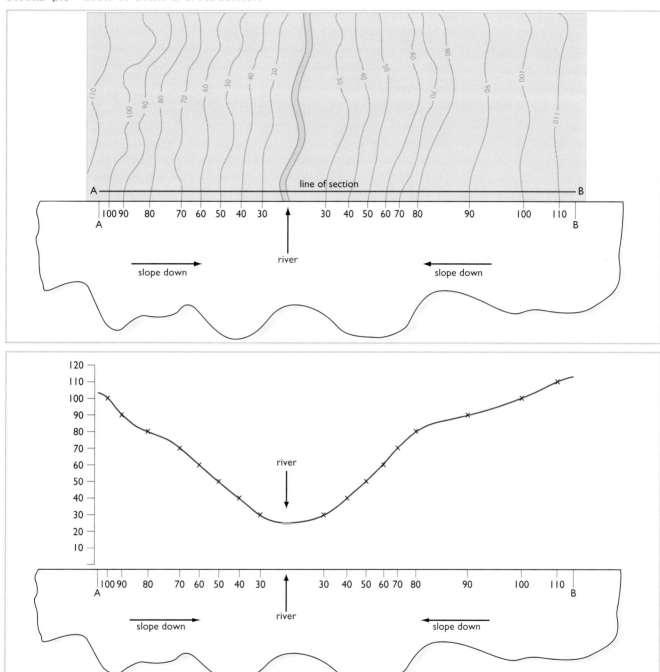

W O R K S H O P

1 Using base map Figure 3.7, draw the cross-sections: X–Y and W–X.
2 Which cross-section has the widest flood plain?
3 Suggest why there is a difference between the two cross-sections.
4 Draw a long profile from the source, A–B.
5 a) Measure the length of the river to the nearest kilometre.

b) Calculate the gradient of the river. To do this:
   i) measure the length of the river;
   ii) work out the difference in height from the beginning of the profile to the end;
   iii) divide the distance by the height.
6 Describe the long profile from A to B.

3.2a *Four figure references*

Introduction

A four figure grid reference locates a grid square on a map. The Ordnance Survey (OS) maps use a National Grid. This is a network of numbered reference lines that covers Great Britain. These lines form 100 km × 100 km squares within which are 10 km × 10 km squares. Each 10 km × 10 km square is divided into 1 km × 1 km squares. These squares can be identified by using a four figure reference.

Giving a four figure reference

Figure 3.9 shows a numbered grid. The numbers across are called **eastings**. Those running up are called **northings**. The shaded square is identified where the easting intersects the northing. Eastings are given first, then the northing. The shaded square is 45 37.

FIGURE 3.9 *Using a four figure reference*

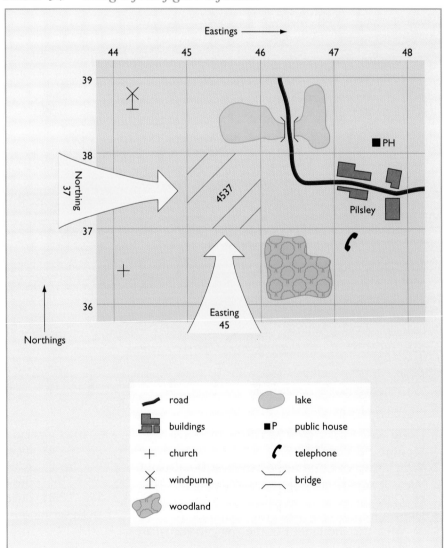

Using a four figure reference

Four figure references can be used to locate places and features, e.g. on Figure 3.9 Pilsley village is at 47 37. They are useful when locating and comparing areas, such as different parts of an urban area or the upper and lower course of a river valley, or for the **population density**.

The buildings of a settlement make up different shapes. The key describes three settlement shapes: loose knit, nucleated (or compact) and linear (Figure 3.10). Grid reference 63 22, Keyes, is an example of a nucleated settlement. In 57 22, Coton is a linear settlement, whereas in 62 19 and 63 20 the settlement is loose knit.

WORKSHOP

1 Using Figure 3.9, identify the features at: (a) 44 38; (b) 46 36; (c) 47 38; (d) 47 36.
2 What is the grid reference for: (a) the woodland? (b) the lake?
3 Using Figure 3.10, identify the settlement shape for each reference: (a) 59 23; (b) 60 20.
4 Study the Bushmills map. Give a four figure reference for each of these settlements and describe their settlement shape: (a) Bushmills; (b) Portballintrae; (c) Leeke.
5 Use other map extracts to give examples of settlement shapes.

WORD BOX

easting the numbered grid line that runs across the map, west to east
northing the numbered grid line that runs up the map, south to north
population density the number of people living in a given area, e.g. one square kilometre

FIGURE 3.10 *Settlement shapes*

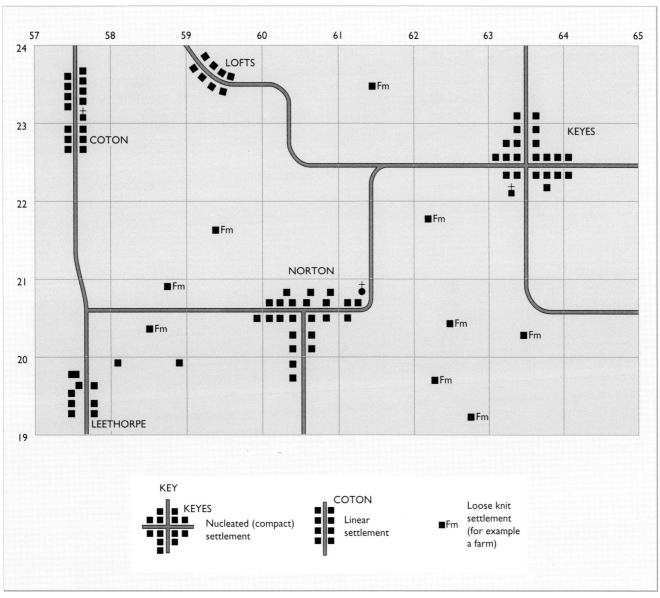

3.2b Six figure references

Introduction

Four figure references only take you to a square kilometre, which is quite a large area. A six figure reference locates an area of 100 m by 100 m and provides a more exact reference. For example, in Figure 3.11 there are two churches in grid square 20 11. The church with a tower is at 203 112. The church with a spire is at 206 117. Each six figure reference is made up of the easting plus a third number, which is the approximate distance across the grid square in tenths. This is an imaginary line. The last part of the six figure reference is the northing plus the approximate distance up the grid square in tenths.

FIGURE 3.11 *How to give a six figure reference*

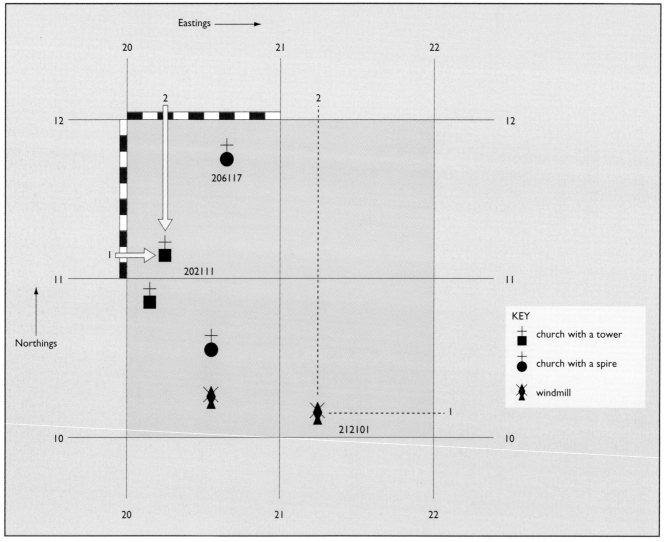

Giving a six figure reference

Figure 3.11 describes how to give the six figure reference of a windmill. First locate the easting before the windmill, easting 21. A third number of the easting reference is given by estimating the number of tenths across the grid square – here 2/10ths. Repeat the same to find the northing, 10 1.

1 Draw a copy of base map Figure 3.12. On your copy plot the following:

    a)   quarry, 0076
    b)   woodland, 0276, 0376, 0475
    c)   lake, 0473, 0176
    d)   golf course, 0574

2 On your base map copy plot the following:

    a)   church with a tower, 030741
    b)   church with a spire, 038729
    c)   windmill, 054714
    d)   public house, 036745
    e)   post office, 031731
    f)   club house, 051743
    g)   level crossing, 025727

FIGURE 3.12 *Base map*

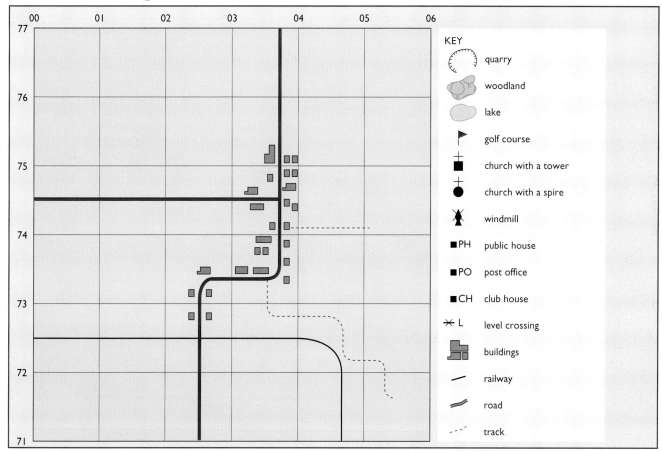

3 Six figure references can be useful in identifying features along a journey. Using the Earith extract (Extract 6), copy and complete the paragraph by writing in the feature found at each reference.

    Leaving (426825) Farm, travel south east along the A142. Cross the (436814) River and (438810) Drain to the road junction at 441803. Turn north east into Mepal. Stop at (441812) for lunch, then at (440807) to pay a telephone bill. Rejoin the A142 going south east to the roundabout at 452793, turn north into the (453798) Park for a job interview. Back to the roundabout to join the B1381. This road goes through the village of (4479). This is a small village but has a (445793), (443788) and (448790). Pass through the village travelling south west to Earith. The village is on a low hill. The height is (377746). This drops to only (429785) and (411767). At the junction of the B1381 and A1123, I stop at the (393746) by the marina to go fishing.

4 Choose another map extract, and write a similar paragraph with grid references for someone else to answer.

3.3a *Scale on maps*

Introduction

Maps are not as large as the area that they represent (Figure 3.13). To draw a map of an area accurately a map scale is used. This tells us how much the real distance between places has been reduced.

Cartographers will choose a map scale suitable for the purpose of the map. When a detailed map of a small area, such as a town centre, is needed a large scale map will be drawn.

When a large area is being shown there is less detail and symbols are used to show important features. A small scale map means a map of a large area, such as a 1:50 000 Ordnance Survey map. This has a scale of 2 cm to represent 1 km.

FIGURE 3.13 *The British Isles shown at a range of scales*

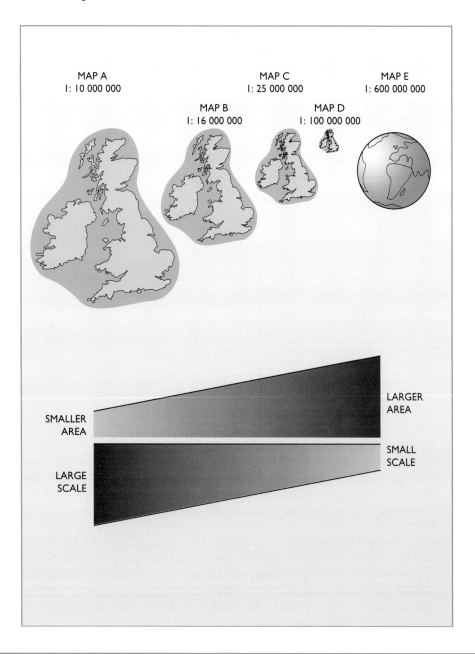

MAP A
1: 10 000 000

MAP B
1: 16 000 000

MAP C
1: 25 000 000

MAP D
1: 100 000 000

MAP E
1: 600 000 000

SMALLER AREA

LARGER AREA

LARGE SCALE

SMALL SCALE

How scale is shown

On a map the scale can be described in one of three ways:
  a) A statement of scale, for example '4 cm represents 1 km' or '1 cm represents 10 m'.
  b) A **scale line**, which is a divided straight line or bar drawn at the bottom of the map.
  c) As a ratio 1:25 000 or 1 to 25 000, or as a fraction 1/25 000. As the scale gets smaller, the ratio or fraction gets larger. This is known as the **representative fraction**.

Map A in Figure 3.13 has a scale of 1:10 000 000. This means 1 cm on the map has a real distance of 100 km. This is calculated by multiplying the map distance by the scale.
  Multiply map distance by map scale:
  1 cm × 10 000 000 = 10 000 000 cm
  Divide by 100 to find out how many metres:
  10 000 000/100 = 100 000 m
  Divide by 1000 to find out how many kilometres:
  100 000/1000 = 100 km

W O R K S H O P

1   Copy and complete the scale details for map A shown in Figure 3.14a.
2   Complete the scale details for map D shown in Figure 3.14b by working out the real distance.
3   Look in an atlas for examples of map scale. Note down examples you find and give the statement of scales (1 cm 5 _____ km).

W O R D   B O X

cartographer   a person who draws maps
representative fraction   the map scale as a fraction
scale line   a line used to show real distance on a map

FIGURE 3.14A   *Scale lines*

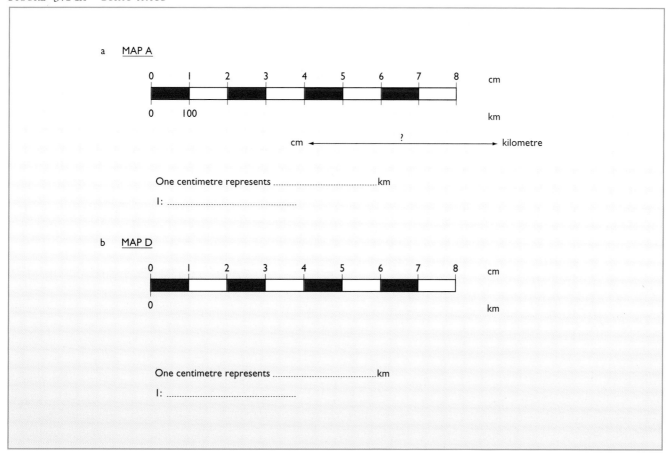

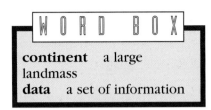

W O R D   B O X

continent   a large
landmass
data   a set of information

3.3b Topological maps

Introduction

A topological map is drawn using **data**. The map does not show proper
distances or shapes. Figure 3.15 shows a topological map based on
world population. The rough shape of each **continent** has been kept,
but the size has been drawn according to the size of its population.
The higher the population, the larger the continental shape. Compared
to Africa, Europe has a higher population. Australia has the lowest
population and the smallest area on the map.

FIGURE 3.15   *Topological population map*

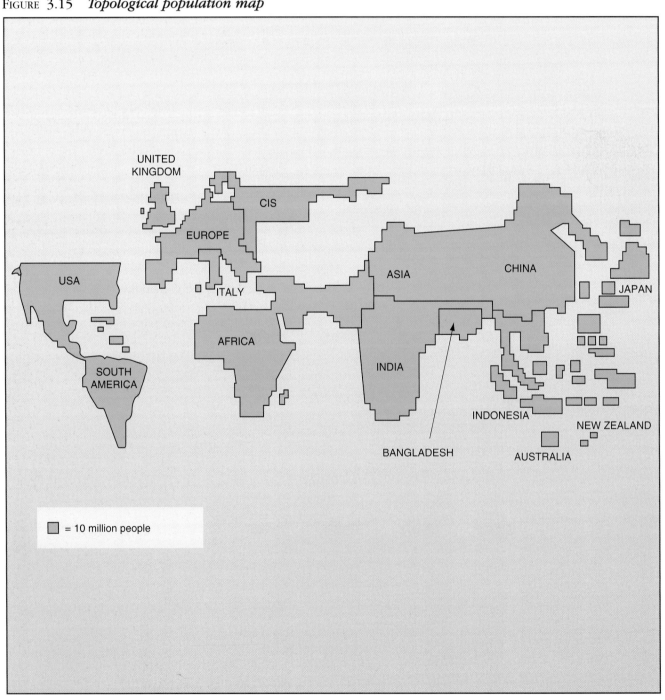

Using satellite photographs

The pressure for farmland and development affects the environment. Satellite images are used to monitor the damage caused by **deforestation**. Large scale deforestation in Brazil may cause changes to the global climate. The unique rainforest ecosystem will be destroyed and lost. Conservationists use a variety of satellite images to monitor and describe the deforestation. Monitoring by satellites shows the process of deforestation (Figure 5.21). Images can be used to show changes in an area over time. Figure 5.22 shows where slash and burn has cleared land for cattle ranching. The image is two frames taken a month apart then combined to show surface cover changes. The new grass growth is green, while the land burnt since is shown as red. Black shows previously cleared areas with no new growth. Figure 5.23 shows how the forest has been cleared as red patches of one square kilometre over a three-year period. The dark areas show previous deforestation.

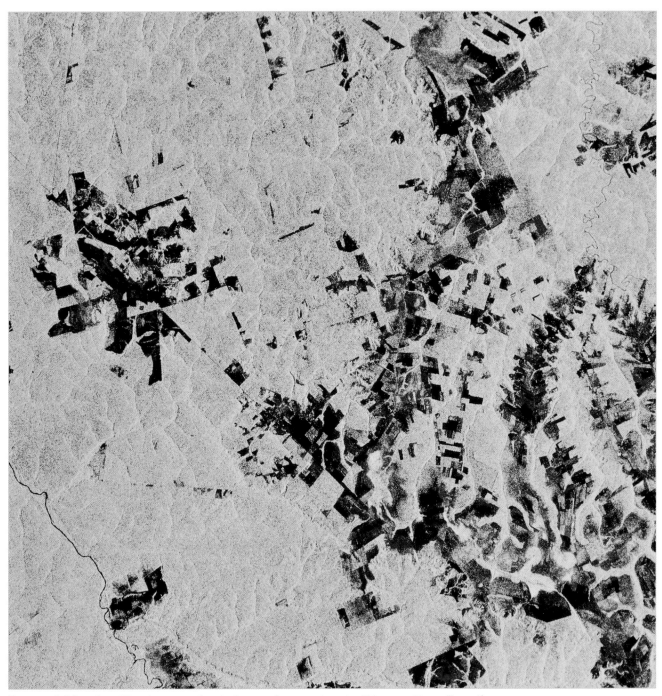

FIGURE 5.22 *Satellite image of rainforest destruction in Diamantina, Brazil*

3.4a *Straight line distances*

Introduction

Straight line distance is the shortest route between two places. Once the map scale is known the distance between places can be worked out. For example, in Figure 3.18 the statement of scale is 4 cm represents the real distance of 1 km, the two farms shown are 8 cm apart. The real distance is 2 km.

Figure 3.20 shows a partially completed distance matrix. The real straight line distance between each place has been measured and recorded as a table. This can then be used as a quick reference.

FIGURE 3.18 *Map extract*

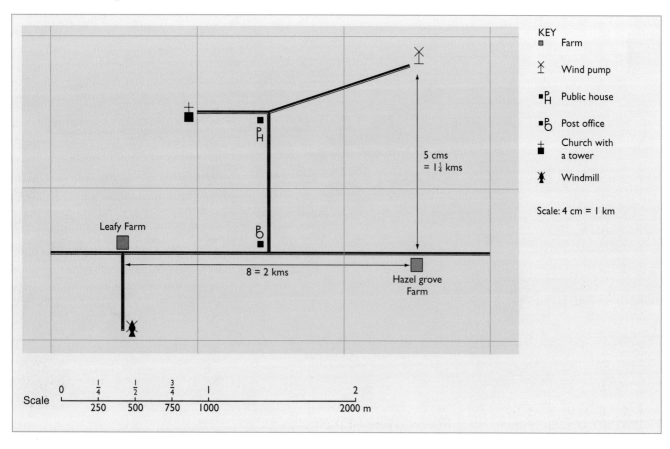

KEY
- ▪ Farm
- ⅄ Wind pump
- ▪P͞H Public house
- ▪P͞O Post office
- ✚ Church with a tower
- ✶ Windmill

Scale: 4 cm = 1 km

5 cms = 1¼ kms

Leafy Farm

8 = 2 kms

Hazel grove Farm

Scale 0   ¼   ½   ¾   1   2
       └──┴──┴──┴──┴──┴──────────────────┴──
          250 500 750 1000   2000 m

Measuring distance

Distance between places on the map can be measured using a piece of paper. Mark the start and end of the route. The real distance can be worked out by placing the paper along the scale line (Figure 3.19). Another way is to use a ruler to measure the distance then change the cm to km using the **scale line**.

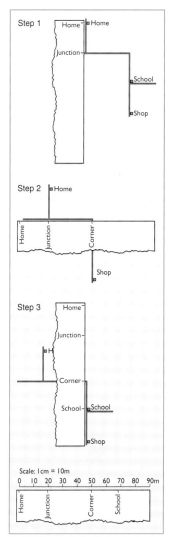
FIGURE 3.19 *Measuring distance along straight line sections*

FIGURE 3.20 *A recording matrix*

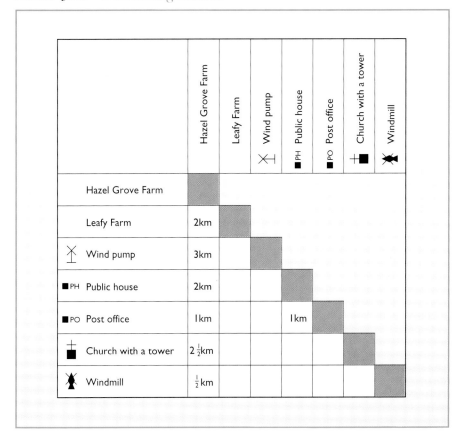

	Hazel Grove Farm	Leafy Farm	Wind pump	Public house	Post office	Church with a tower	Windmill
Hazel Grove Farm							
Leafy Farm	2km						
Wind pump	3km						
Public house	2km						
Post office	1km		1km				
Church with a tower	2½km						
Windmill	½km						

WORKSHOP

1 Complete the matrix (Figure 3.20) by measuring the missing distances on Figure 3.18.
2 Using the Montego Bay map (Extract 2), measure the straight line distance from the hotel at grid reference 207638 to these attractions:
 a) the cricket ground, 215620
 b) the football ground, 214630
 c) the church, 223627
 d) the fort, 207627
 e) Gunpoint Wharf, 208623
 f) the library, 208627
 g) Cornwall Beach, 205634.
3 Repeat the measurements from the hotel at grid reference 214626.
4 Which hotel can claim to be most **accessible** for these attractions?

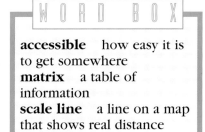
WORD BOX

accessible how easy it is to get somewhere
matrix a table of information
scale line a line on a map that shows real distance

CHAPTER 6
Using Information Technology

6.1 *Using Information Technology (IT)*

Introduction

IT has many uses in geography. These two pages will help you to make the most of IT in school and as part of coursework/fieldwork. Figure 6.1 lists some of the main uses of IT. Figure 6.2 gives some of the main reasons for using IT. Figure 6.3 shows some of the IT resources that you could use. There are other things you could use as well. For example, there are digital cameras and Geographical Information Systems (GIS) that combine maps with huge databases of statistics and photographs.

FIGURE 6.1 *What can you use IT for?*

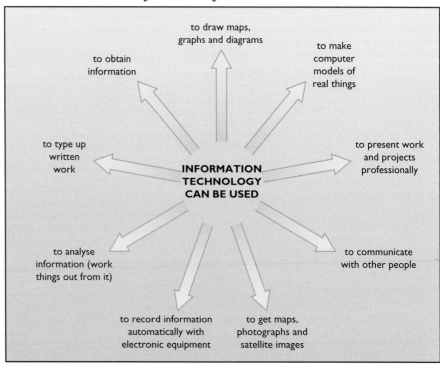

to draw maps, graphs and diagrams

to obtain information

to make computer models of real things

to type up written work

INFORMATION TECHNOLOGY CAN BE USED

to present work and projects professionally

to analyse information (work things out from it)

to communicate with other people

to record information automatically with electronic equipment

to get maps, photographs and satellite images

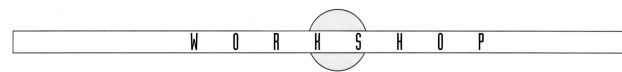
W O R K S H O P

1 Make a list of the things you have used IT for in geography already.
2 What, if any, IT resources do you have: (a) at home; (b) at school in the geography classroom/area; (c) at school in the library/Resources Centre; (d) in your local library; (e) in the main library.
3 Think back over the work you have done in geography during the last six months. Write about two things that you could have used IT for.
4 Write about two things that you would like to use IT for in the next six months.

FIGURE 6.2 *Why use IT?*

- **It helps you to do some things much more quickly, e.g. drawing a graph. This gives you more time to think about the geography.**

- **It is easy to change things on a computer, so drafting and re-drafting, and experimenting with different types of graph, for example, becomes possible.**

- **It allows you to handle an enormous amount of data so that you can answer more questions, more fully.**

- **It can make some things, such as shading in a map, much easier.**

- **It lets you do many things that simply are not possible without a computer, e.g. using the Internet.**

FIGURE 6.3 *IT word box*

WHAT?	WHAT FOR?	EXAMPLE
database	recording, analysing and presenting data (words and numbers)	a database of development indicators
spreadsheet	recording mainly numbers in a table, carrying out calculations and presenting data	working out the population of a country in 50 years time
word processor	writing text	typing a report about an earthquake
Desk Top Publishing package	putting together text, maps, graphs, photographs etc as a finished piece of work	presenting an account of an oil spill with a map and photographs as well as a typed report
'Draw' programme	drawing maps and diagrams; adding to / changing maps, diagrams and photographs	drawing a flow diagram of the hydrological cycle; using graded shading to show levels of unemployment in different countries
CD-ROM	finding out information from a computerised encyclopaedia, large database, collection of photographs etc.	playing a geographical game about the growth and development of a city
Internet	searching for information on the World Wide Web	searching for up to date information about rainforest destruction
E-mail	swapping messages and data with other people anywhere in the world	swapping weather data with schools in other countries
data logger	automatically collecting data	collecting soil and air temperature for a 24 hour period

3.5a *Eight points of the compass*

Introduction

To find a place you can give directions using a compass. Figure 3.23 shows the eight points of the **compass**.

FIGURE 3.24 *Damage caused by the eruption of Mount St. Helens*

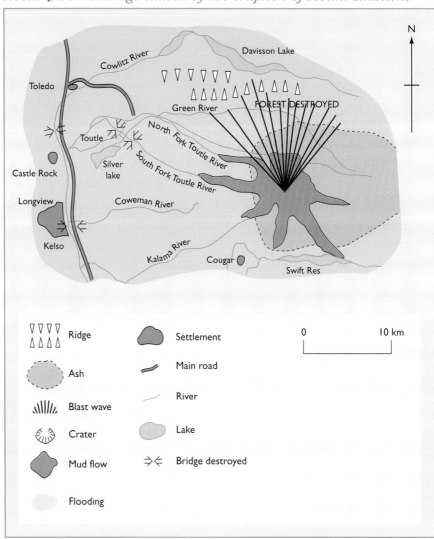

FIGURE 3.23 *Eight points of the compass*

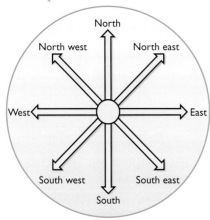

Giving a direction

Direction is given with the compass point away from where you are. When Mount St Helens erupted it blasted hot ash, dust and gases out northwards. The blast travelled very quickly, destroying everything in its path. Hot **lava** slowly flowed in various directions away from the crater. Figure 3.24 maps the damage caused by the eruption.

CHAPTER 3

WORKSHOP

1 If a compass was placed at point A on Figure 3.25, which volcanoes would be found at each of the compass points?

2 Use Figure 3.24 to copy and complete the paragraph by writing in a compass direction.

   Mt St Helens erupted on the 18 May 1980. The main blast was to the _____. It destroyed 250 km of forest. The eruption melted snow and caused mud flows _____ along the North Fork Toutle River, _____ along the South Fork Toutle River, and _____ _____ along the Kalama River. The mud flows caused flooding along the valleys and towns to the _____ of Mt St Helens.

3 Scientists have made predictions about a future eruption of Mt St Helens. On an outline of Figure 3.24 show that:
   a) the blast will be between north west and the south;
   b) the lava will flow from two openings in the volcanic cone, one between east and south east, and a second between south west and west;
   c) the wind will blow clouds of ash and gas west of the volcano;
   d) the rivers north and east of the volcano will flood with mud and snow meltwater.

FIGURE 3.25 *Locating volcanoes*

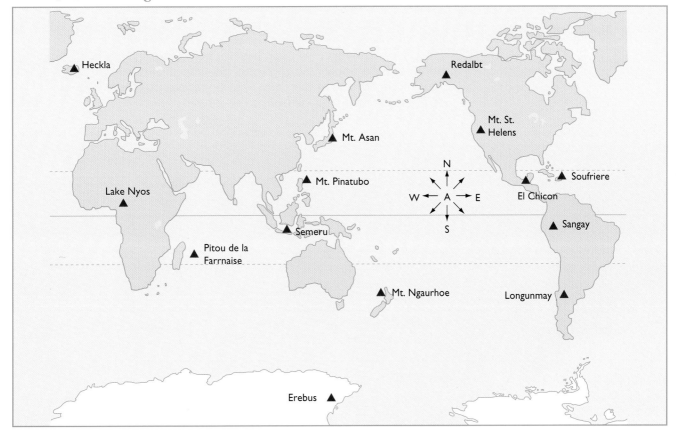

4 Use your completed map to describe which areas and towns would be affected by the eruption of Mount St. Helens.

Databases 2

Introduction

Setting up your own database is quite straightforward, but you have to go through a number of stages very carefully (Figure 6.6).

The first question you have to ask yourself is 'Should I be using a database?'. If you want to sort out certain facts from large amounts of data, e.g. all of the earthquakes greater than 7 on the Richter scale since 1970, or all of the settlements in the UK with a population of more than 1 million, as well as present and analyse that information, then the answer is 'yes'. However, if you only want to present the information and/or to analyse it, another tool, such as a graphics package or a spreadsheet, might be better.

The next stage is to plan the database with pencil and paper – it will save time in the long run! What fields are you going to include? Is the data in the form of numbers or letters? How do you want the display to look? You may have to give 'short names' for the fields: do these names make sense? Is the information available for all records?

You are now ready to set up a blank record. Save it and give the database a name. Enter data for the first four or five records, save it and try it out. Does it work as you had intended, or are some of the fields unnecessary? Do the 'short names' need changing? It is very unusual to get a database right first time, but trying it out means that you can change it before you have spent hours inputting data.

When the database is how you want it to be, enter the data for all of the records. Save regularly so that the chances of losing data are slight: typing errors and other mistakes are easy to change.

Your database is now ready to use. If it is a good database it will allow you to do a large number of things that would take ages to do 'long hand'. However, you still have to be a geographer to get the most out of it so do not forget important geographical questions such as Where is it? What is it like? How did it get like that? How is it changing? What will it be like in the future?

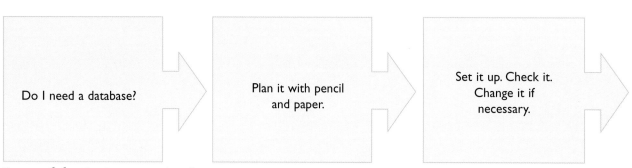

FIGURE 6.6 *Setting up a database*

WORKSHOP

1 Set up a database of social and economic **indicators** for 25 countries. An atlas and/or a digest of geographical statistics are likely to be good sources of information.
   - Ten of the countries should be **MEDCs** and 15 of the countries should be **LEDCs**. Use the **North–South Development Line** to separate MEDCs from LEDCs.
   - Each record should have nine fields – one of these will be the name of the country and one will be whether it is an MEDC or LEDC but you must choose and research the other seven fields (indicators).
2 When you have set up your database and entered all of the information, print out one of the records.
3 Try out all of the functions of your database.
4 Use the graph and/or statistics function to draw scatter graphs to see if there is a relationship (correlation) between any of the indicators (see pages 24–25). If you do find a correlation, try to explain it.
5 Write an account of your database project:
   - Describe what you were asked to do.
   - On an outline map of the world, mark on and label your 25 countries.
   - Explain why you chose your indicators. Did they turn out to be good indicators?
   - Write down at least ten things you have learnt from your database.
   - Include any graphs that you have drawn. Add labels to explain what they show.
   - Write a short evaluation of the project. Did you enjoy it? Give reasons.

WORD BOX

indicators statistics that tell us something about a place, e.g. how economically developed it is

LEDCs Less Economically Developed Countries: the poorer countries of, mainly, South America, Africa and Asia

MEDCs More Economically Developed Countries: the richer countries of, mainly, North America and Europe

North–South Development Line an imaginary line that separates MEDCs from LEDCs, which you will find in most atlases

---

Enter the data.
Save regularly.
Check the entries.

Use it to answer important geographical questions, e.g.
Where is it?
What is it like?
How did it get like that?
How is it changing?
What will it be like in the future?

3.5c Bearings

Introduction

Compass **bearings** are based on the 360 degrees in a circle. A degree is not a distance but a measure of turn. Bearings are used to give an exact direction between two places. The amount of turn is always clockwise from north; the number of degrees turned is called the bearing (Figure 3.30). A bearing can be measured using a circular protractor or a graduated compass.

FIGURE 3.30 *Reading a bearing*

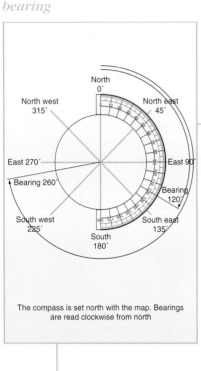

The compass is set north with the map. Bearings are read clockwise from north

FIGURE 3.31 *South Downs Route*

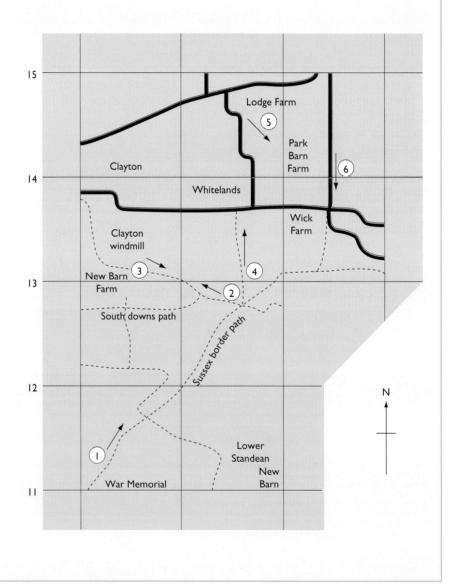

6 To Wick Farm

5 To Park Barn Farm

4 To Whitelands and Lodge Farms

3 Paths meeting

2 To Clayton WindMills

1 Paths meeting

Bearings for each point

Using bearings

A series of bearings can provide an accurate route to be followed. Figure 3.31 shows a route based on the OS map (Extract 5a), South Downs, which uses bearings. A **landmark** or grid reference can be used to provide a start and finish to each part of the route.

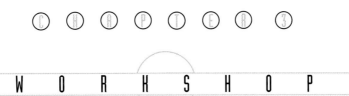

1 Figure 3.31 is a sketch map based on the South Downs map (Extract 5a). For each section of the route shown, give the bearing.
2 Figure 3.32 shows a simple orienteering map. Plot a route using bearings to find the quickest circular route around the course visiting each of the checkpoints. Use tracing paper to plot the route and mark the compass bearings to follow. Remember that straight lines are usually the best route, but you need to avoid obstacles.
   a) Use the compass or protractor to work out the best route.
   b) Measure the distance between each checkpoint.
   c) Compare your route to others in your class: can you improve your route?

FIGURE 3.32 *Orienteering map extract*

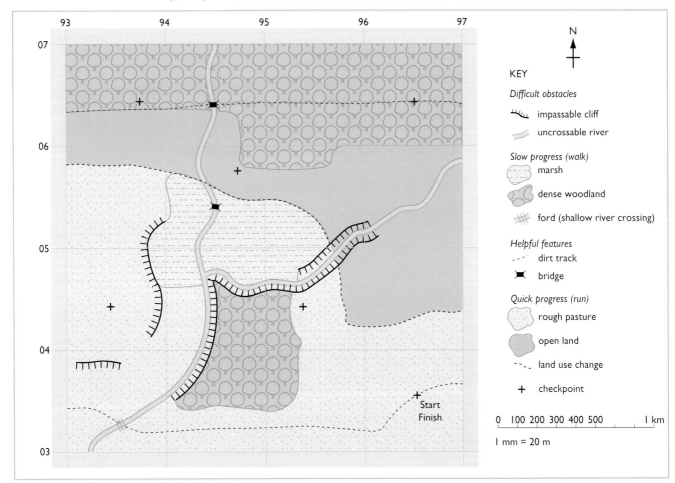

3 Use the Bushmills OS map (Extract 1) to describe a route using bearings along the North Antrim Cliff Path from the car park at Dunluce Castle, 902411, to Portmoon House, 974455.

WORD BOX

bearing a number of degrees from north
landmark an important feature

6.4 *Spreadsheets*

Spreadsheets 1

Introduction

A spreadsheet can be used to record any geographical information that can be set out as a table. Each box in the spreadsheet is known as a **cell**. You can type words and numbers in the cells and then use the spreadsheet to draw graphs. You can also type **formulae** into the cells and use the spreadsheet to carry out calculations.

There are many different spreadsheets programs, but they all work in much the same way. The main features of a spreadsheet are shown in Figure 6.8.

FIGURE 6.8 *An example of a blank spreadsheet*

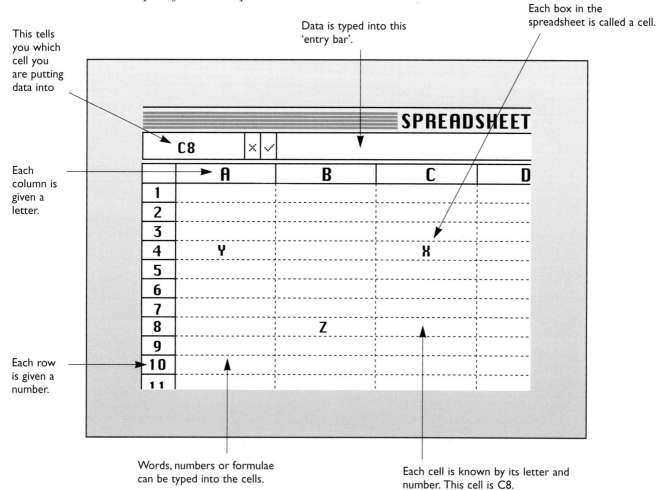

This tells you which cell you are putting data into

Data is typed into this 'entry bar'.

Each box in the spreadsheet is called a cell.

Each column is given a letter.

Each row is given a number.

Words, numbers or formulae can be typed into the cells.

Each cell is known by its letter and number. This cell is C8.

WORKSHOP

1 Look at Figure 6.8. Write down the **co-ordinates** of cells X, Y and Z.
2 a) Figure 6.9 shows a spreadsheet set up with the populations of the countries in the European Union. Follow the instructions for the spreadsheet on your computer and set up a spreadsheet like this one.
  b) Use your spreadsheet to draw a bar chart of these figures.
  c) Use your spreadsheet to draw a pie chart of these figures.
  d) Cell B15 has worked out the total population of the countries of the European Union. Change the figure for the United Kingdom in cell B1 to 100. What has happened to the total population figure in cell B15?
  e) Can you find figures that are more up to date than 1993? If you can, you could enter them into the spreadsheet and the total would be automatically updated. You could redraw your graphs in a few seconds as well!

WORD BOX

cell   a box in a spreadsheet into which you can type words, numbers or formulae
co-ordinates   a way of identifying a square
formulae   a set of mathematical symbols for carrying out a calculation

FIGURE 6.9   *European Union population spreadsheet*

EU POPULATION

| B15 | ✕ | ✓ | =SUM(B1..B14) |

	A	B	C	D
1	UK	58		
2	Ireland	4		
3	Denmark	5		
4	Greece	11		
5	Italy	57		
6	France	58		
7	Netherlands	15		
8	Belgium/Luxembourg	11		
9	Germany	82		
10	Spain	40		
11	Portugal	11		
12	Austria	8		
13	Sweden	9		
14	Finland	5		
15	Total (millions)	374		
16				

The formula to add up the total population of the countries has been typed into cell B15. Different spreadsheets use different formulae, so check your instructions.

3.6b Describing a micro-climate

Introduction

A **micro-climate** is a variation in local weather conditions. These differences are caused by local factors such as buildings, aspect or vegetation. To investigate whether a micro-climate existed, a route around a school was planned. Four observations about the weather were made at each of the 12 stops.

Plotting a transect

A thermometer recorded temperature, a wind streamer identified wind direction and a hand held **anemometer** measured wind strength. Care was taken with the readings and all observations about the surroundings were noted. A comment about that day's general weather conditions was also made (Figure 3.35).

FIGURE 3.35 *Transect around the school*

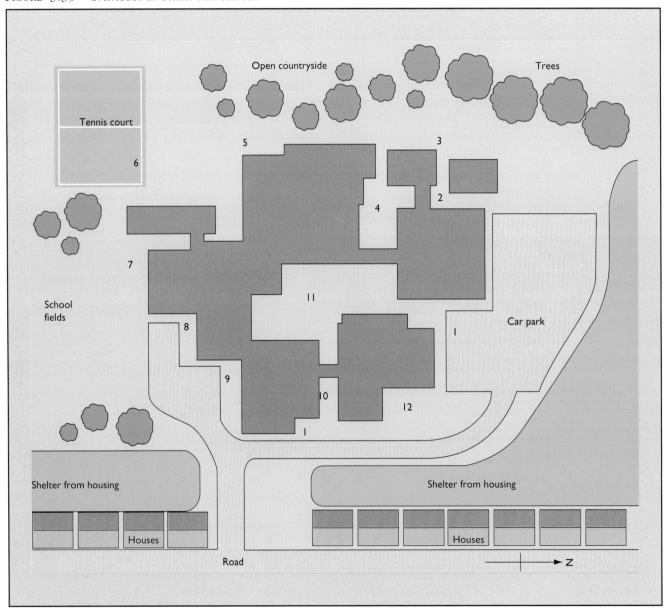

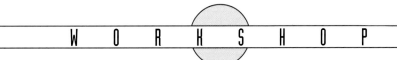

1 Use Figure 3.35 and 3.36 to complete the following tasks: (a) make a copy of the school map; (b) label the 12 stops; (c) for each stop write the temperature; (d) for each stop draw a line to represent the wind direction (use a scale of 1 cm per unit of wind speed).

2 Look at your completed map. Describe which parts of the school are: (a) the warmest and coolest; (b) most windy and calmest.

3 What is the school's micro-climate? Explain your answer.

4 Choose an idea for a local transect. These are some examples:
  ● house age: the age of housing increases towards the centre of a town;
  ● field land use: grazing land is found on the steepest slopes;
  ● footpath usage: footpath erosion occurs where there is greatest use;
  ● litter: the most litter is found near shops.

Write an action plan using the following headings:

a) Aim: describe what you are going to investigate, think of a hypothesis (idea) to investigate.

b) Method: prepare a base map and a key for recording information on your base map.

c) Fieldwork: undertake your fieldwork.

d) Presentation and comment on findings: present your findings as a map and write a description of your transect.

e) Analysis and explanation: describe the main differences along your transect. Did your findings prove or disprove your original idea?

f) Evaluation: how do you think you could improve your transect?

g) Conclusion: what have you found out, what else could be investigated?

FIGURE 3.36 *Micro-climate data*

Stop.	Max. Temp.	Wind Speed	Wind Direction	General comments
1	19	5	NE	Car park in shadow
2	10	3	N	Between buildings
3	11	4	N	Slight shadow
4	12	2	SW	Wind swirling, some shadow
5	11	4	NW	Sunny, strengthening wind
6	10	6	NW	Exposed on tennis courts
7	13	2	NW	Shelter from buildings, sun trap
8	14	Calm	–	Sheltered by building
9	12	5	NE	Sheltered by building
10	12	7	N	Wind funnelled between buildings
11	12	6	N	Wind swirling
12	10	6	NE	Sheltered, shadow

Time taken : 10. 30 am
Date : 10 May
Weather : Bright skies, winds from North-Northwest

anemometer an instrument for measuring wind speed
aspect the direction a slope is facing
micro-climate the climate of a small area caused by local factors

6.5 *Draw and paint programs*

Draw 1

Introduction

Draw and Paint programs are very useful in geography for drawing maps and diagrams. There are many different types of Draw and Paint programs but they all work in much the same way. Figure 6.12 shows how a Draw program can be used to present a flow diagram. Figure 6.13 shows how a Draw program can be used to label a map.

FIGURE 6.12 *Drawing a flow diagram: the erosion of a headland*

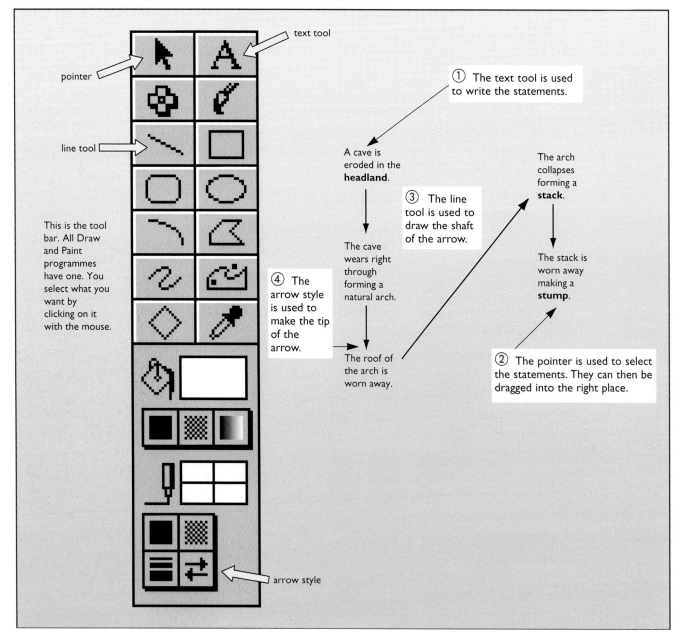

Detailed recording along a transect

Detailed observations about the river were made at eight survey points. Some notes were made about the river between these stops to help with the follow up work. Measurements and observations about the appearance of the river were made at each stop (Figure 3.38).

FIGURE 3.38 *Data collected from the transect*

STOP	MILL LANE	COALITE	STORFORTH LANE	HASLAND ROAD	CHESTERFIELD CANAL	BRIMINGTON	BARROW HILL	STAVELEY
Land use %	100% farmland	80% derelict factory site 20% farmland	60% industry 40% open space	30% allotment 50% industry 20% housing	70% industry 30% open area and canal	30% derelict land 40% industry 30% housing	90% housing 10% derelict land	40% farmland 40% industry 20% derelict land
evidence of wildlife	9/10	4/10	2/10	4/10	5/10	3/10	4/10	6/10
vegetation	10/10	4/10	4/10	6/10	5/10	4/10	4/10	7/10
noise level	8/10	5/10	4/10	4/10	3/10	4/10	5/10	6/10
damage / litter	8/10	3/10	4/10	3/10	4/10	4/10	5/10	6/10
attractiveness	9/10	3/10	3/10	3/10	5/10	6/10	3/10	6/10
river colour	clear, 10/10	clear, 10/10	reddy-brown 1/10	red with oily skim 3/10	dark but clear dust / oil on surface 5/10	clear 8/10	oil and dust on surface 5/10	foam, oil and dust on surface, discoloured 3/10
ph colour	7	8	8	6	8	8	8	8

Higher the score out of 10, the better the feature : 10/10 excellent, 5/10 satisfactory, 1/10 poor.

W O R K S H O P

1 Using Figure 3.38:
   a) describe how the land use changes between stop 1 and stop 8;
   b) describe how the environmental quality changes between stop 1 and stop 8.
2 What evidence suggests that there is a link between the land use and environmental quality?
3 Using the information available about the transect, write up the results as a report. Use these headings and suggested presentation.
   a) Aim: What was the aim of this work? Suggest an appropriate hypothesis.
   b) Method: Explain how the data was collected.
   c) Presentation: Draw a map locating the area. For each stop draw a chart to show the quality of environmental factors. For each stop draw a pie chart to show land use.
   d) Analysis and explanation: Describe how the environmental quality changes along the transect. Suggest reasons for these changes.
   e) Evaluation: Suggest the possible limitations of this investigation. How might the investigation be improved?
   f) Conclusion: What factors seem to have an affect on the environment?

W O R D   B O X

environmental quality an assessment of how good or poor an area is
pH value a number that represents how acidic or alkaline the water is

3.7a *Simple relationships: height and rainfall*

Introduction

Maps can be used to investigate **relationships** between various geographical **patterns**. Examples of using maps to identify relationships include settlement growth, how settlement patterns have been influenced by relief, the accessibility of service centres, and farming land use with geology and relief. By comparing details on a map or with other maps, relationships between features can be identified.

Height and rainfall

An investigation of a hill farm may identify several relationships. For example, land use and distance from the farm. Dairy cows and grazing may be closer to the farm than arable crops or rough pasture. Other relationships could include a link between climate and relief, land use and slope or aspect. Relief rainfall (Figure 3.39) suggests that the higher the land, the greater the annual rainfall.

FIGURE 3.39 *Relief rainfall*

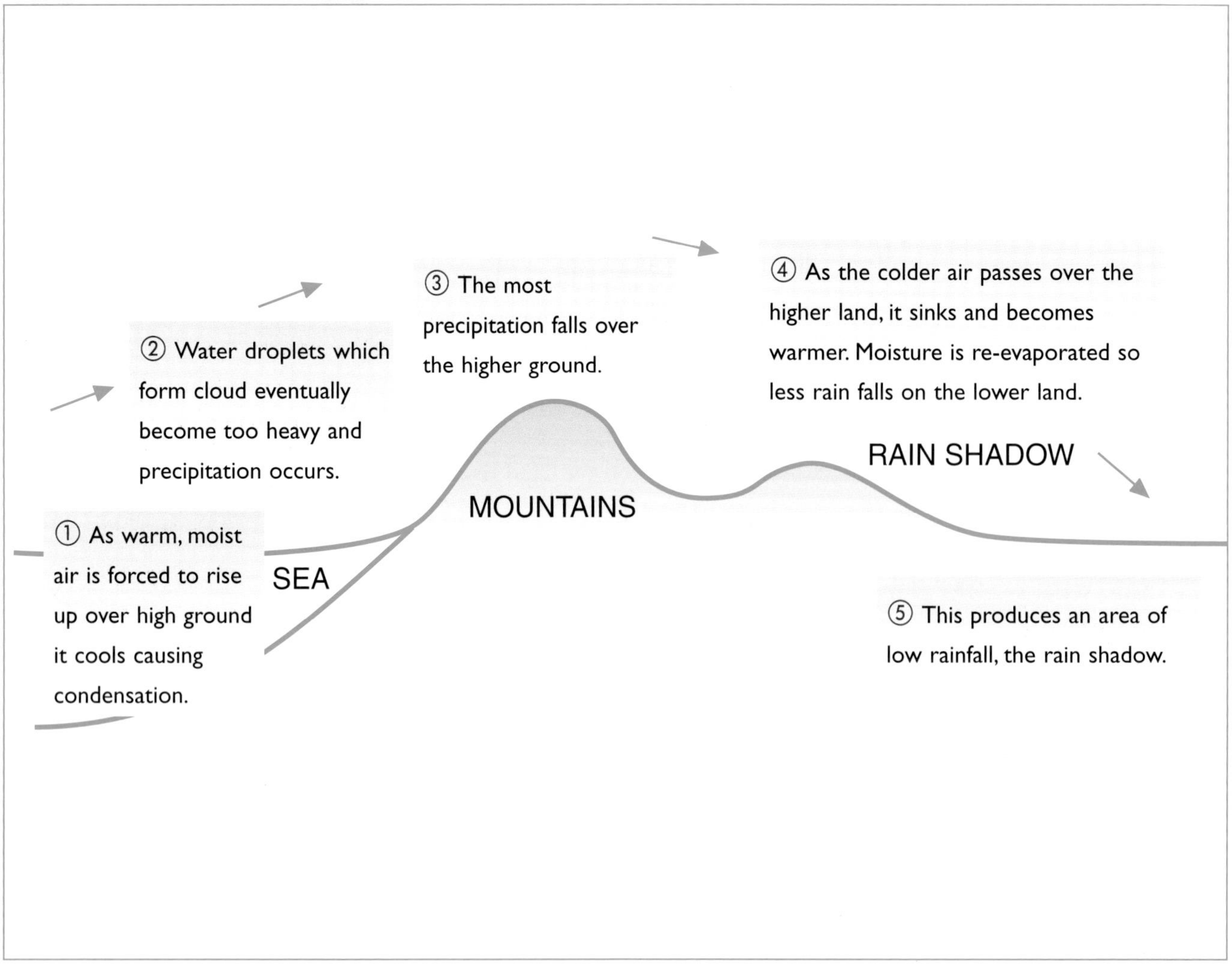

② Water droplets which form cloud eventually become too heavy and precipitation occurs.

③ The most precipitation falls over the higher ground.

④ As the colder air passes over the higher land, it sinks and becomes warmer. Moisture is re-evaporated so less rain falls on the lower land.

RAIN SHADOW

MOUNTAINS

① As warm, moist air is forced to rise up over high ground it cools causing condensation.

SEA

⑤ This produces an area of low rainfall, the rain shadow.

WORKSHOP

1 a) Draw a copy of the map in Figure 3.40.
  b) Complete the **isohyets**.
  c) Describe the relationship between height and rainfall.

FIGURE 3.40 *Base map*

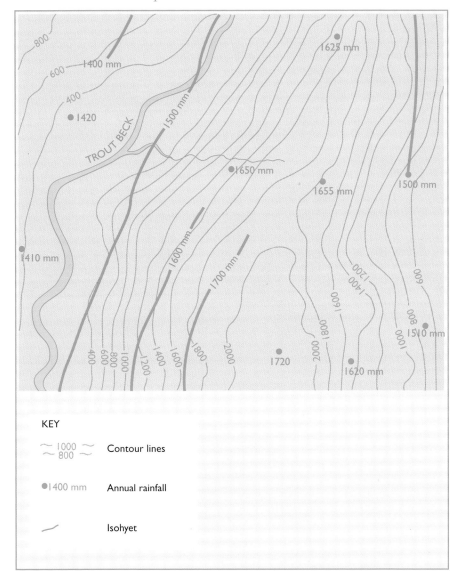

KEY

≈ 1000 ≈
   800   Contour lines

●1400 mm   Annual rainfall

⟋   Isohyet

1	Achnashellach	1 500mm
2	Edinburgh	700mm
3	Inverness	700mm
4	Fort William	2 000mm
5	Oxford	600mm
6	Keswick	1 500mm
7	Ifracombe	900mm
8	Nairn	600mm
9	Wick	800mm
10	York	700mm
11	Tynemouth	700mm
12	Blaenau Ffestiniog	2 000mm
13	Llandrindod Wells	1 000mm
14	Buxton	1 500mm
15	Skegness	500mm
16	Birmingham	700mm
17	Southampton	700mm
18	Gorleston	400mm
19	Cambridge	500mm
20	Weymouth	800mm

FIGURE 3.41 *Selected climate stations annual rainfall (rainfall figures have been simplified)*

WORD BOX

isohyet a line that joins up places with equal rainfall
relationship a link between geographical features
pattern a distribution of a geographical feature, e.g. rainfall

2 a) Use an atlas to locate the climate stations in Figure 3.41.
  b) On an outline map of Great Britain write on the rainfall total for each station.
  c) Draw isohyets for: 1400 mm; 1500 mm; 1600 mm; 1700 mm.
3 a) On your map shade in the following highland areas: Lake District, Pennines, Welsh mountains, Dartmoor, Exmoor and North Yorkshire Moors.
  b) Describe the relationship between rainfall and relief shown on your map.

3.7b Complex relationships

Introduction

Information from maps can identify more than geographical patterns and relationships. By comparing maps, complex links can be recognised although there may be a common explanation. Figures 3.42 and 3.43 suggest that there is a climate change inland from the coast. The temperature and **precipitation** maps and data (Figure 3.44) also suggest a seasonal pattern.

FIGURE 3.42 *European annual rainfall*

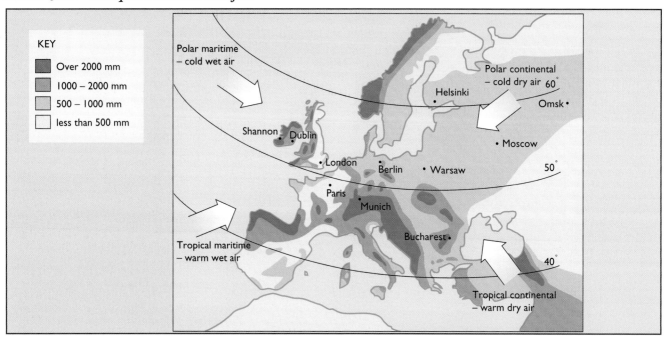

FIGURE 3.43 *European isotherms for July and January*

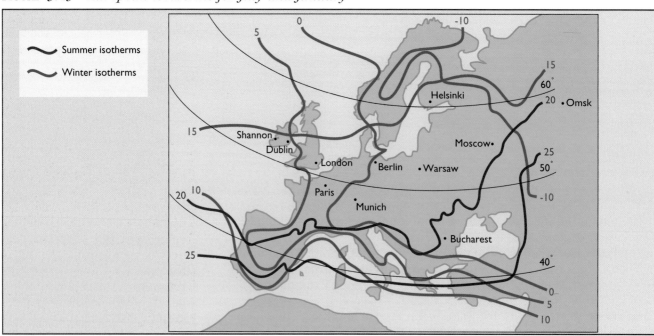

Climatic influences

The climate of northern Europe is affected by various air masses. **Maritime** influences from the Atlantic Ocean, especially the North Atlantic Drift, have an important effect on the climate. Sea areas take longer to warm up than land, but the sea water retains its warmth into the colder winter months. Coastal areas experience milder winters. Away from the coast, the climate is influenced by the continental land mass rather than the ocean. The land warms and cools quickly. The temperature range increases inland. In summer the longer days mean the land becomes very warm, but the shorter winter days give low temperatures.

FIGURE 3.44 *Climate data for selected European Stations*

Station	Average temp.	Hottest month temp.	Coolest month temp.	Temperature range
Berlin	9	19	−1	20
Bucharest	11	30	−7	37
Dublin	12	20	1	19
Helsinki	6	22	−10	32
London	11	18	4	14
Moscow	4	18	−13	31
Munich	9	23	−5	28
Omsk	−1	18	−22	40
Paris	12	20	4	16
Shannon	12	20	3	17
Warsaw	8	19	−3	22

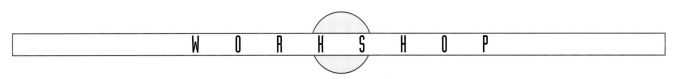

WORKSHOP

1 Using Figures 3.42 and 3.43, describe how rainfall and summer and winter temperature changes along latitude 50N.

2 Using an atlas and the data in Figure 3.44:
  a) plot on a blank map as a bar graph of northern Europe and Russia the average temperature for each station;
  b) annotate your map to describe how the average temperature changes inland;
  c) plot on a blank map as a bar graph of northern Europe and Russia the temperature range for each station;
  d) annotate your map to describe how the temperature range changes inland.

3 Describe how the average temperature and the temperature range changes inland away from the sea.

4 a) Plot the data for the hottest and coolest month on the map.
  b) Describe the seasonal relationship shown.
  c) Suggest reasons for this relationship.

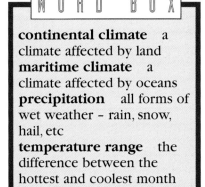

WORD BOX

continental climate a climate affected by land
maritime climate a climate affected by oceans
precipitation all forms of wet weather – rain, snow, hail, etc
temperature range the difference between the hottest and coolest month

Extracts from the key of the 1:50000 OS of Northern Ireland 'Discoverer' Series

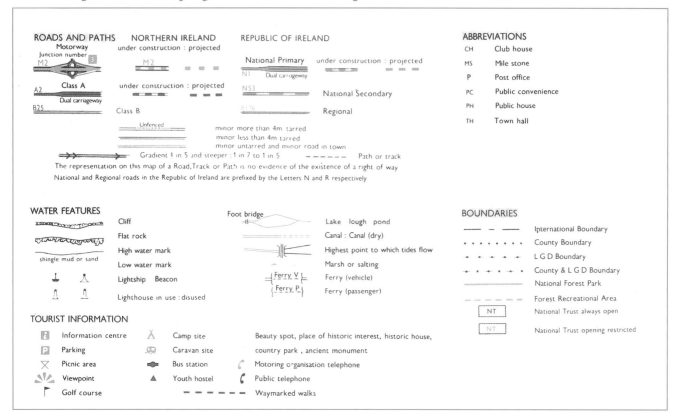

Extracts from the key of the 1:50000 OS 'Landranger' Series

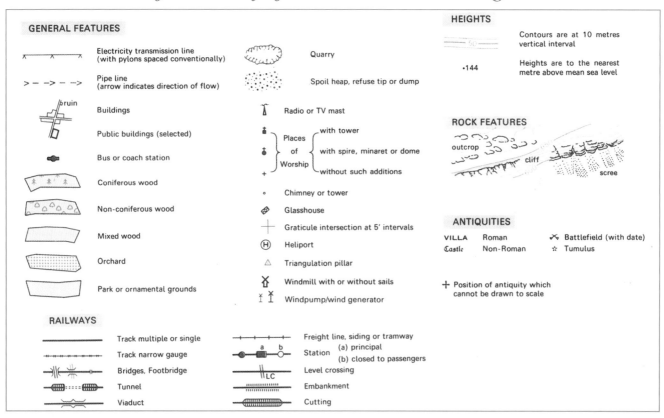

© Crown copyright

C H A P T E R 3

Extracts from the key of the 1:25000 OS of Jamaica

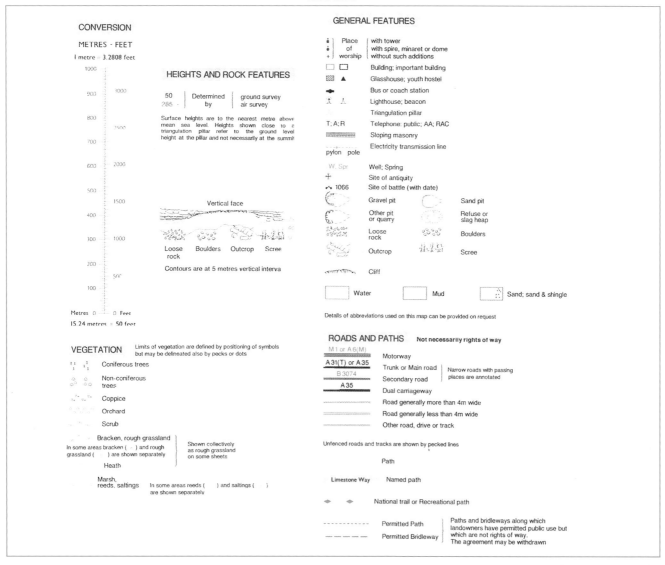

Extracts from the key of the 1:25000 OS of the Peak District 'Outdoor Leisure' series

© Crown copyright

CHAPTER 4
Making Maps

4.1 *Sketch maps*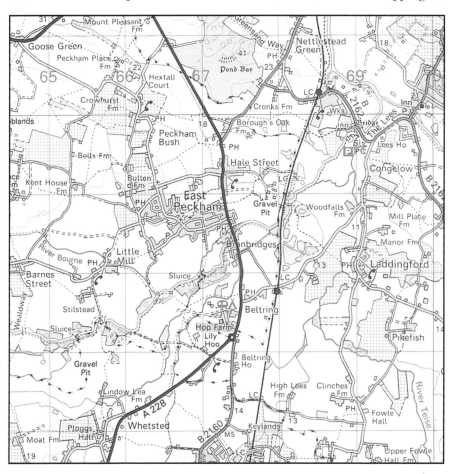

Sketch maps 1

Introduction

One of the most important questions asked in geography is 'Where is it?' One of the best ways of answering this question is to draw a sketch map. You can draw a sketch map of a street, a country or a continent. You can show human features, such as settlements, or physical features, such as rivers. However, the most important thing is to keep your sketch map simple – only show the things you are interested in.

FIGURE 4.1   *OS map extract: East Peckham, Kent (© Crown copyright)*

The OS map extract (Figure 4.1) shows the village of East Peckham in Kent. The village has been built at a **bridging point** on the River Medway. Its **site** is slightly higher ground above the river's **flood plain** (you can tell this from the contour lines). Its **situation** has a number of advantages:

- in the past the river would have provided water and a means of transport;
- it is a **route centre** because of the bridge;
- it is surrounded by fertile land (you can tell this from the symbol for orchards, see page 84).

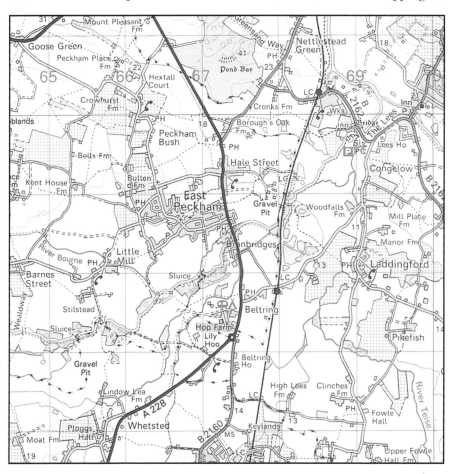

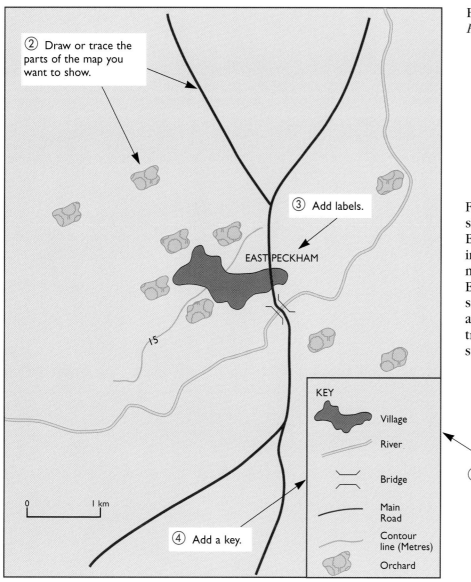

FIGURE 4.2 *Sketch map: East Peckham's site and situation*

② Draw or trace the parts of the map you want to show.

③ Add labels.

EAST PECKHAM

15

① Draw a frame.

④ Add a key.

KEY

Village

River

Bridge

Main Road

Contour line (Metres)

Orchard

0   1 km

Figure 4.2 is a sketch map to show the site and situation of East Peckham. Only the important things from the OS map have been shown. Everything has been kept very simple. If you are not very good at drawing, use a piece of tracing paper to get you started!

W O R K S H O P

1 Label onto a copy of Figure 4.2 the following words and phrases to show the site and situation of East Peckham: BRIDGING POINT; ROUTE CENTRE; FLOOD PLAIN; HIGHER LAND; FERTILE LAND; RIVER MEDWAY. (Note: your copy does not have to have the 'instructions' 1, 2, 3 and 4 written onto it.)

W O R D   B O X

bridging point   a place where a bridge can be built across a river
flood plain   the area either side of a river onto which it spills when it bursts its banks
route centre   a place where roads and other lines of transport, e.g. rail, sea, air, come together
site   the ground that a settlement, for example, is built on
situation   the area around, for example, a settlement

Sketch maps 2

Introduction

Sketch maps can also be used to show the relationship between features, especially between physical and human features. For example, Figure 4.3 is a sketch map of OS Extract 5a. The main physical feature is the steep chalk scarp slope running east–west across the map. To the south of this is the gentler dip slope while to the north is lower, flatter land.

FIGURE 4.3   *Sketch map of OS Extract 5a: Westmeston*

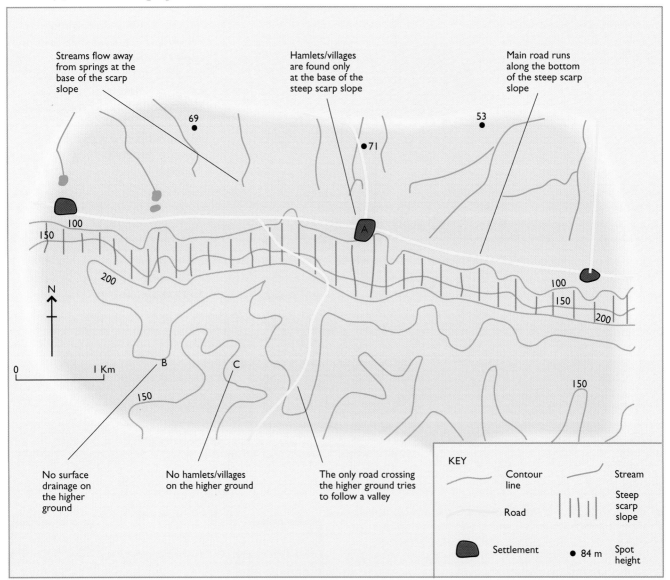

The scarp and dip slope are **permeable** chalk while the land to the north is mainly **impermeable** clay. Some small streams are found to the north of the scarp slope. The main human features are the roads and three small settlements. These physical and human features have been marked onto the sketch map. Relationships between them can then be spotted and explanations can be suggested, e.g. the main road runs along the bottom of the steep scarp slope because it is flatter and lower ground.

1 Look at Figure 4.3. Suggest possible explanations for the relationships labelled A, B and C.

2 Figure 4.4 is the outline for a sketch map of part of OS Extract 1. Onto a copy of this outline:
   a) Shade in the land over 50 metres in height.
   b) Label these physical features: Bush River; an area of the river's **flood plain**; Portballintrae Bay; the sand dunes near Bushfoot Strand.
   c) Label these human features: the settlements of Portballintrae and Bushmills; the bridges across the river in Bushmills; the golf course near Bushfoot Strand.
   d) Identify, and label onto your map, relationships between the following: (i) **relief** and roads; (ii) relief and settlement; (iii) settlement and **bridging points**; (iv) settlement and bays; (v) the golf course and physical feature(s).
   e) Try to explain the relationships you have labelled onto your sketch map.

FIGURE 4.4   *Sketch map outline for OS Extract 1: Portballintrae*

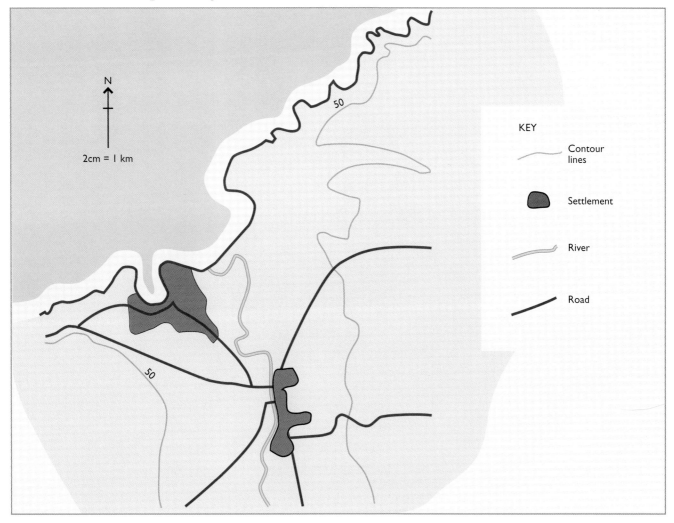

KEY

—— Contour lines

◼ Settlement

—— River

—— Road

N

2cm = 1 km

50

50

4.2 *Graded shading maps*

Graded shading maps 1

Introduction

Graded shading maps are a good way of showing the amount of something in an area. For example, Figure 4.5 shows the number and **distribution** of people living in the counties of Wales. The key is very important. The numbers must go up in equal steps. The shading must go from dark to light so that it is easy to see a pattern. You could also use a graded shading map to show the amount of energy each country uses, or the amount of money it earns.

FIGURE 4.5 *How to draw a graded shading map*

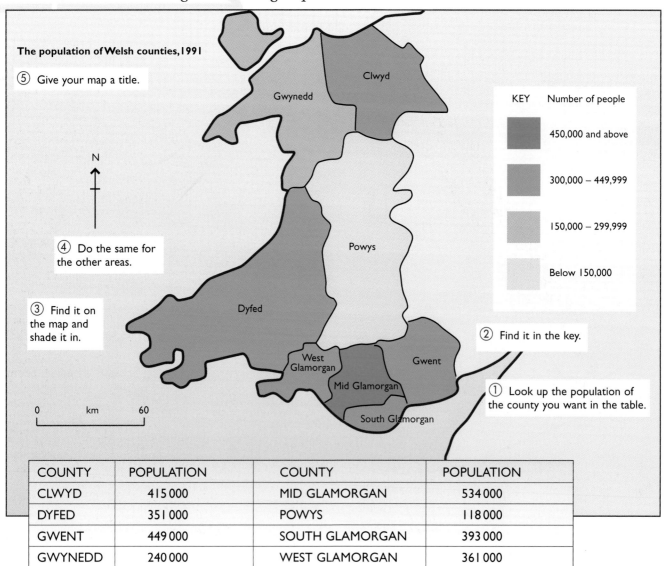

COUNTY	POPULATION	COUNTY	POPULATION
CLWYD	415 000	MID GLAMORGAN	534 000
DYFED	351 000	POWYS	118 000
GWENT	449 000	SOUTH GLAMORGAN	393 000
GWYNEDD	240 000	WEST GLAMORGAN	361 000

W O R K S H O P

1 Look at Figure 4.5. Which county of Wales stands out as having the biggest population?
2 Which county of Wales stands out as having the smallest population?
3 Use the statistics in Figure 4.6, and a copy of the outline in Figure 4.7, to draw a **population density** map of South America. (Look up the names of the countries in an atlas and label them first. Use a number key if the countries are too small for their names to be written on your map, e.g. 1 = Guyana.)
4 Which countries stand out as being the most densely populated?
5 Which countries stand out as being the least densely populated?

W O R D   B O X

distribution   where something is found
population density   the number of people living in a given area, e.g. one square kilometre

FIGURE 4.6   *Population density in South American countries, 1995*

COUNTRY	POPULATION DENSITY
Venezuela	23
Brazil	19
Guyana	4
Bolivia	7
Surinam	3
Paraguay	13
Guiana	2
Chile	18
Colombia	34
Argentina	13
Ecuador	41
Uruguay	18
Peru	18

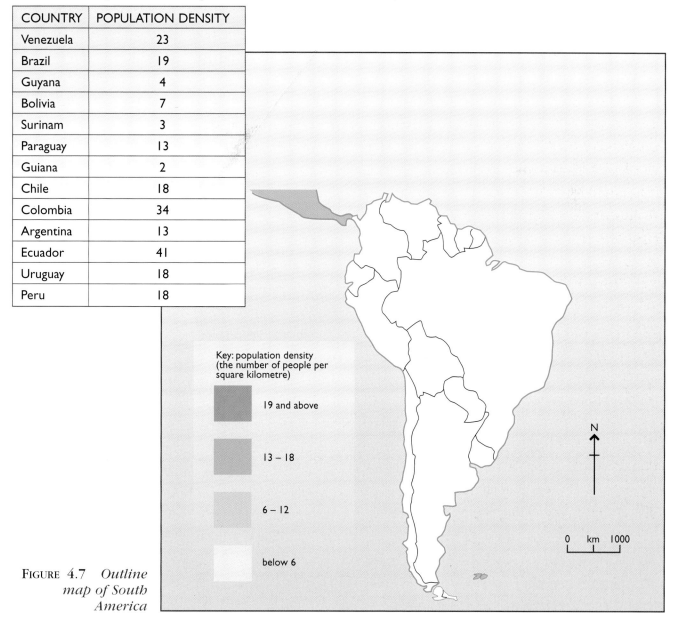

Key: population density
(the number of people per square kilometre)

19 and above

13 – 18

6 – 12

below 6

N

0   km   1000

FIGURE 4.7   *Outline map of South America*

Graded shading maps 2

Introduction

In the Workshop on page 91 you were given the key for the graded shading. However, when you carry out your own **primary** or **secondary data collection** and you want to draw a graded shading map you will have to design your own key. The example in Figure 4.8 gives you some rules to follow. It uses the statistics in Figure 4.9.

FIGURE 4.8 *Working out the key for a graded shading map*

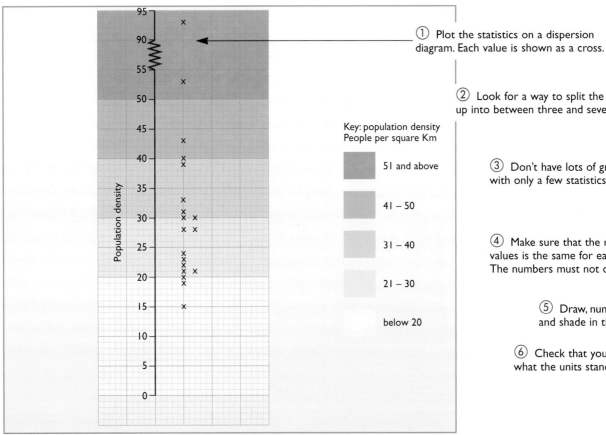

① Plot the statistics on a dispersion diagram. Each value is shown as a cross.

② Look for a way to split the statistics up into between three and seven groups.

Key: population density People per square Km

51 and above

41 – 50

31 – 40

21 – 30

below 20

③ Don't have lots of groups with only a few statistics in them.

④ Make sure that the range of values is the same for each group. The numbers must not overlap.

⑤ Draw, number up and shade in the key.

⑥ Check that you have said what the units stand for.

WARD	POPULATION DENSITY	WARD	POPULATION DENSITY
Abbey	53	Boulton	43
Derwent	22	Mickleover	30
Allestree	19	Breadsall	33
Kingsway	21	Osmaton	30
Alvaston	15	Chaddesden	39
Litchurch	20	Sinfin	21
Babington	93	Chellaston	23
Littleover	31	Spondon	28
Blagreaves	28	Darley	24
Mackover	40		

FIGURE 4.9 *Population density (people per square kilometre) by ward: Derby, 1991*

W O R K S H O P

1 Use the statistics in Figure 4.10, and a copy of the outline in Figure 4.11, to draw a population density map of Inner London. You should draw a **dispersion diagram** first to work out the number of groups. Be careful with your shading method.

FIGURE 4.11 *Outline map of Inner London*

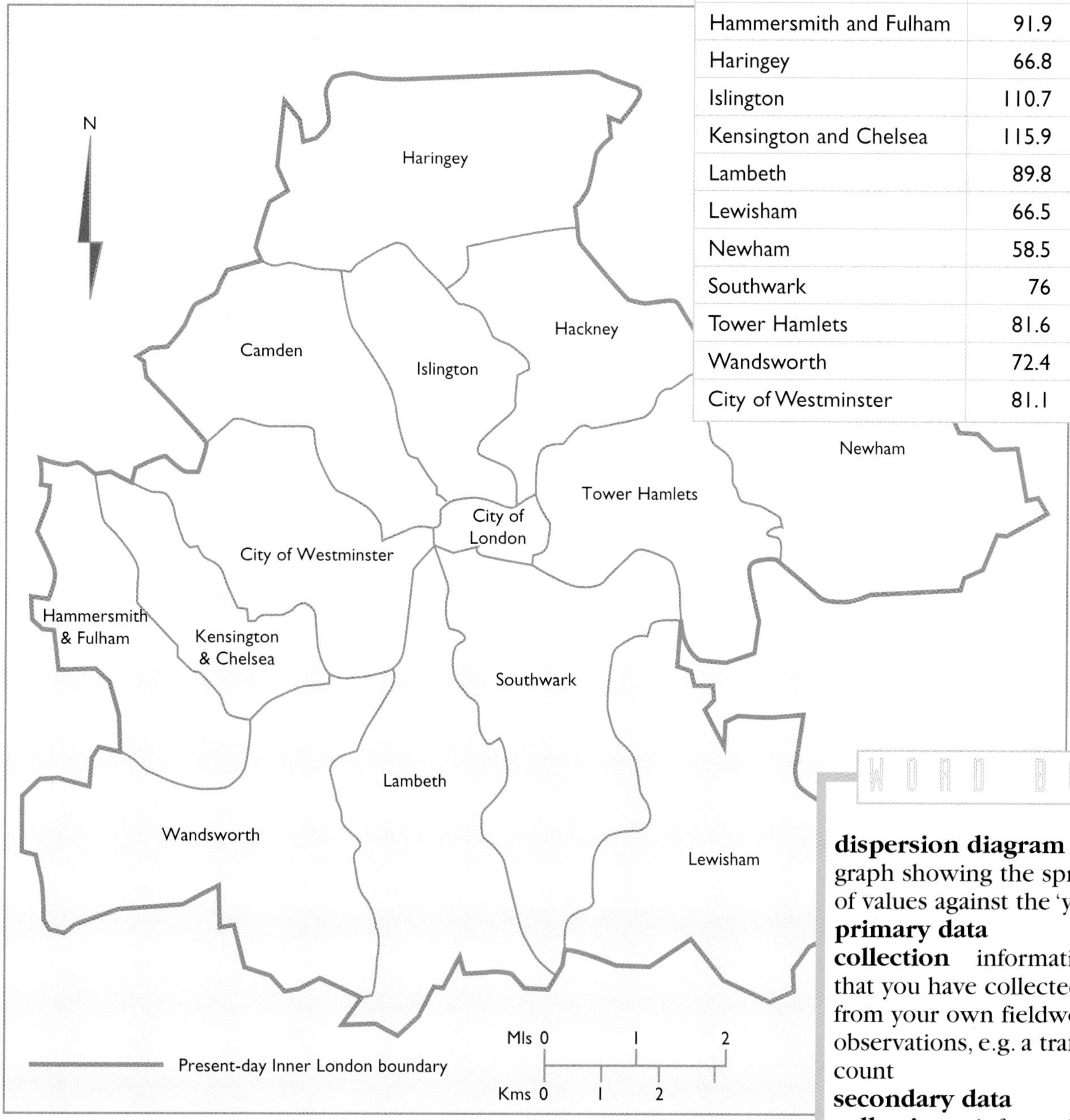

Present-day Inner London boundary

Mls 0   1   2
Kms 0   1   2

FIGURE 4.10 *Population density in Inner London (persons per hectare, 1991)*

BOROUGH	DENSITY
City of London	15.1
Camden	78.5
Hackney	92.9
Hammersmith and Fulham	91.9
Haringey	66.8
Islington	110.7
Kensington and Chelsea	115.9
Lambeth	89.8
Lewisham	66.5
Newham	58.5
Southwark	76
Tower Hamlets	81.6
Wandsworth	72.4
City of Westminster	81.1

W O R D   B O X

dispersion diagram a graph showing the spread of values against the 'y axis'
primary data collection information that you have collected from your own fieldwork observations, e.g. a traffic count
secondary data collection information you have collected from, for example, a text book or the census

2 Describe the pattern shown on your map.
3 Try to explain the pattern on your map.
4 What would you expect to happen to population densities as you move away from Inner London towards the outskirts, and why?

4.3 *Isoline maps*

Isoline maps 1

Introduction

Isolines join places of equal value. Contours on an OS map are an example of isolines: they join places of equal height. Isobars on a weather map are another example: they join places of equal pressure. Isolines are a good method to use if you have data for a great many points in an area. For example, Figure 4.12 uses isolines to join places of equal earthquake intensity (measured on the **Mercalli scale**). This earthquake happened near Naples in Italy in November 1980. Settlements near the **epicentre** suffered most damage. In total 3000 people died and half a million buildings were destroyed.

FIGURE 4.12 *How to draw an isoline map*

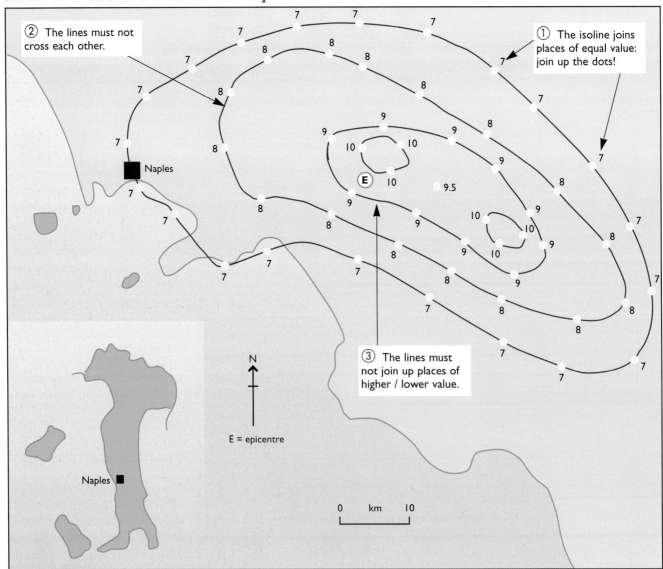

1 The force of an earthquake gets less as you move away from the epicentre. In October 1989 an earthquake measuring 7 on the **Richter scale** occurred to the south of San Francisco in California. Figure 4.13 shows how the force of this earthquake became less with distance. San Francisco was shaken by only 10 per cent of the earthquake's original force, but this was still enough to claim 270 lives and cause $10 billion of damage.

   a) Draw onto a copy of Figure 4.13 the 60, 40, 20 and 10 per cent isolines. Each line has been started for you.

   b) Describe the pattern your map shows.

   c) Study a map of California. Suggest reasons why most of the damage was in San Francisco, even though it was a long way from the epicentre.

W O R D   B O X

epicentre the place on the surface above where an earthquake starts (its focus)
Mercalli scale a scale from 1 (least) to 12 (most) that describes the damage caused by an earthquake
Richter scale a scale from 0 to 8.9 that measures the energy released by an earthquake

FIGURE 4.13 *The 1989 San Francisco earthquake*

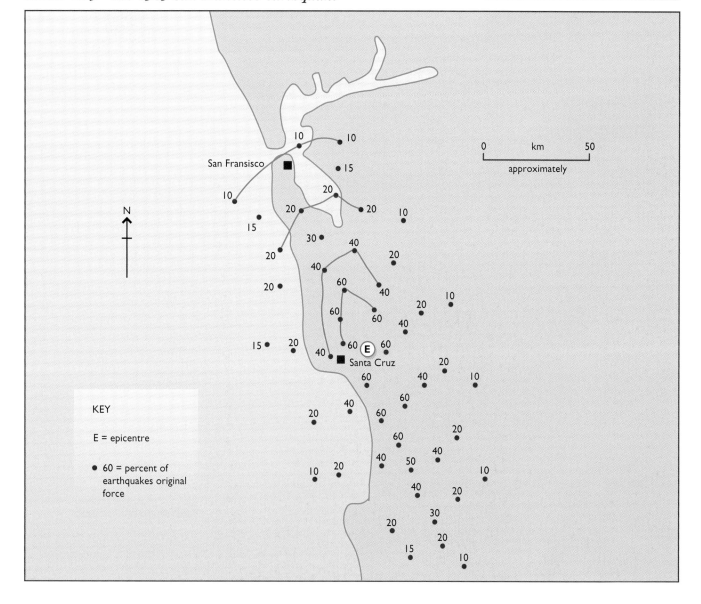

Isoline maps 2

Introduction

To draw an isoline map you need to work carefully through four main stages:

- Stage 1 Mark the data onto your base map in pencil. Remember, the more data you have, the more accurate your finished map will be.
- Stage 2 Decide on the values for the isolines. Do this by looking at the range of values, plotted onto a dispersion diagram if at all possible. For example, Figure 4.14 is a dispersion diagram of the temperature data shown on Figure 4.15. The range is quite small (13.5–18°C) and the intervals between the values is very regular (half a degree Celsius). You could choose to have five isolines at degree intervals, or 10 at half degree intervals. Your decision does not matter as long as you have enough isolines to show a pattern and as long as the interval between them is always the same.
- Stage 3 Draw the isolines onto your base map in pencil. Remember the rules described on page 94.
- Stage 4 When you are happy with the pattern, ink in the isolines and number them. Check that you have completed the key.

(Note: Graded shading (see pages 90–93) can be used between the isolines to emphasise the pattern.)

FIGURE 4.14 *Dispersion diagram of the temperature data on Figure 4.15*

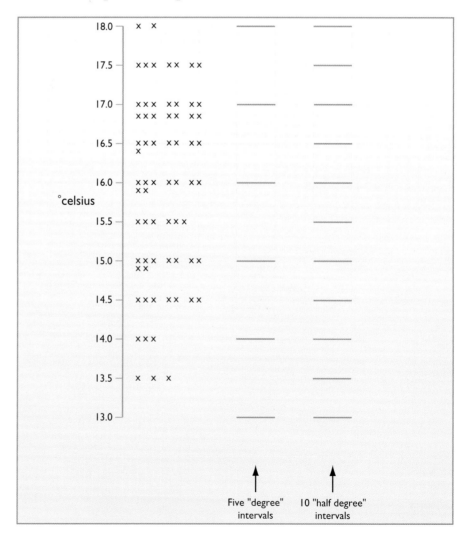

W O R K S H O P

1 Work in pairs for this exercise. Draw isolines onto a copy of Figure 4.15. One of you should use degree intervals and the other half degree intervals. Compare your finished maps. How are they similar? How are they different?

2 Describe the pattern shown on your finished map. Try to explain it.

3 'Iso' comes from Isos, the Greek word for equal. Read through the names given to the different types of isoline map in the word box. Find examples of these in your atlas.

4 What other types of data in the atlas are shown with isolines?

FIGURE 4.15 *July isotherms in the UK*

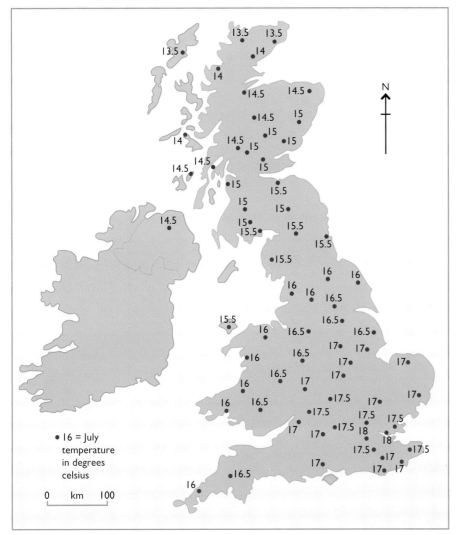

```
• 16 = July
  temperature
  in degrees
  celsius

0    km   100
```

4.4 *Dot maps*

Dot maps 1

Introduction

A dot map is a good way of showing where something is found (**distribution**). Each dot stands for a certain value and the dots should all be of the same size. They can be spread evenly throughout the area or, if you have enough information, you can put them in their 'real' place. Drawing the dots can be quite difficult so it is best to use a stencil. For example, Figure 4.16 is a dot map to show the amount of forest in Britain in 1990. You could also draw dot maps to show the distribution of a country's population.

FIGURE 4.16 *How to draw a dot map*

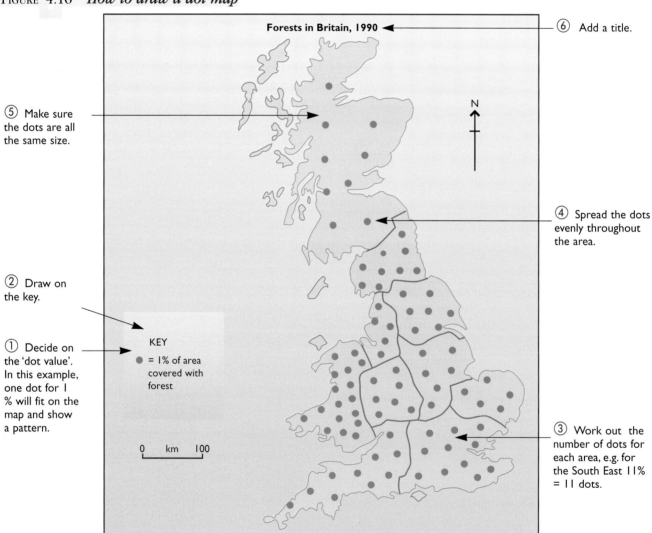

⑥ Add a title.

Forests in Britain, 1990

⑤ Make sure the dots are all the same size.

④ Spread the dots evenly throughout the area.

② Draw on the key.

KEY

● = 1% of area covered with forest

0   km   100

① Decide on the 'dot value'. In this example, one dot for 1 % will fit on the map and show a pattern.

③ Work out the number of dots for each area, e.g. for the South East 11% = 11 dots.

W O R K S H O P

1 (You will need copies of Figures 4.17 and 4.18 for this activity.) Draw a dot map to show the distribution of forests in Europe. To do this:

a) Finish Figure 4.17 so that you know how many dots you need for each country. Use a scale of one dot = 5 per cent. The first country has been done for you.

b) Use an atlas to help you label the countries.

c) Draw on the dots. Each dot should have a **diameter** of 3 mm. Place the dots evenly, or if your atlas gives you information about where the forests are found in each country, draw them on their right places.

d) Check that your map has a key and a title.

e) Describe the pattern your map shows. (Which countries have the most forest? Which have the least?)

f) Suggest reasons for the pattern your map shows. (Is it to do with **relief**, climate, population, land use?)

FIGURE 4.17   *Forests in Europe*

COUNTRY	FORESTED AREA (%)	NO. OF DOTS (1 dot = 5%)
UK	10	2
Ireland	5	
Norway	25	
Sweden	70	
Denmark	10	
Germany	30	
Netherlands	10	
Belgium/ Luxembourg	20	
France	25	
Spain	30	
Portugal	30	
Italy	20	
Switzerland	25	
Austria	40	

FIGURE 4.18   *Outline map of Europe*

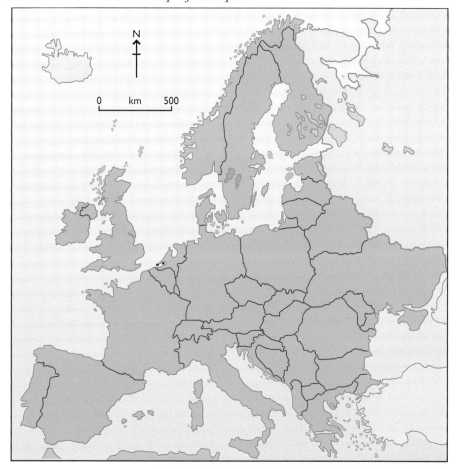

W O R D   B O X

diameter the distance across a circle, passing through the centre
distribution where something is found
relief the height and shape of the land

Dot maps 2

Introduction

Working out the 'dot value' has to be done with great care. If the dot value is too small you will end up with too many dots to mark on the map. If the dot value is too large you will have too few dots and the map will not show a pattern. The best way to tackle this problem is to set out the data in a table like the one in Figure 4.19 and then experiment with different dot values. 'Rounding up' and 'rounding down' will also be necessary. You will need to take into account the base map you will be using and you will also need to experiment with the size of dot.

FIGURE 4.19   *Deciding on a dot value*

① The activity here is to draw a dot map to show car production for the world's top ten producers (1993).

COUNTRY	CAR PRODUCTION (thousands)	NUMBER OF DOTS
JAPAN	8682	9, 17 or 35?
USA	5700	
Germany	3926	
France	2921	
South Korea	1628	
Spain	1506	
UK	1375	
Italy	1310	
Canada	1100	
Russia	1000	1, 2 or 4

② A dot value of 1000 would be alright for Japan (8682 / 1000 = 8.68, = 9 dots 'rounded up'). However, the bottom four countries would have only one dot each which would not show much of a pattern.

③ A dot value of 250 would be alright for the bottom 6 countries, e.g. Russia would be 1000 / 250 = 4, = 4 dots. However, it would mean 35 dots for Japan which would take a long time to draw and would definitely not fit within the country on the world map.

⑤ 17 dots for Japan is still quite a large number, so on an A4 world base map a dot size of 3 mm should be the maximum.

④ A dot value of 500 produces an acceptable result. Japan gets 17 dots while Russia gets 2.

W O R K S H O P

1 (You will need a world base map for this activity.)
  a) Draw a dot map to show car production for the world's top ten producers (see Figure 4.19), using a dot value of 500 and a dot size of 3 mm.
  b) Describe and comment on the distribution shown on your map.
2 a) Draw a dot map to show steel production for the world's top ten producers (Figure 4.20).
  b) Describe and comment on the distribution shown on your map.
  c) Compare your map of world car production with your map of world steel production. Are there any similarities? What could explain these?

FIGURE 4.20 *World steel production, 1993*

COUNTRY	STEEL PRODUCTION (million tonnes)	No. of DOTS
JAPAN	99.6	
CHINA	88.6	
USA	87	
RUSSIA	59	
GERMANY	37.6	
UKRAINE	35	
SOUTH KOREA	33	
ITALY	25.8	
BRAZIL	25.8	
CANADA	24.9	

FIGURE 4.21 *World sugar cane production, 1993*

COUNTRY	SUGAR CANE PRODUCTION (thousand tonnes)	No. of DOTS
BRAZIL	251408	
INDIA	230832	
CHINA	68419	
CUBA	44000	
MEXICO	41652	
PAKISTAN	38743	
THAILAND	34710	
INDONESIA	32400	
AUSTRALIA	31700	
COLOMBIA	30500	

FIGURE 4.22 *World sugar beet production, 1993*

COUNTRY	WORLD SUGAR BEET PRODUCTION (thousand tonnes)	No. of DOTS
UKRAINE	33717	
FRANCE	31748	
GERMANY	28610	
RUSSIA	25500	
USA	23946	
POLAND	15621	
TURKEY	15563	
CHINA	12100	
ITALY	11867	
UK	8988	

3 a) Draw dot maps to show world **sugar cane** (Figure 4.21) and world **sugar beet** (Figure 4.22) production. (You could show both on the same map using different coloured dots, but you will need to use different scales.)
  b) Describe and explain the distributions shown on your map(s). Why are the distributions different?

W O R D   B O X

sugar beet a root crop that likes moderate temperatures and rainfall
sugar cane a tall grass with a thick stem, which likes a hot, wet climate
(Note: both are important sources of sugar.)

4.5 *Flow line maps* £

Flow line maps 1

Introduction

A flow line map is a good way of showing movement from one place to another. Figure 4.23, for example, shows traffic on a main road counted by a Year 7 class in a 15-minute period of time. The width of the arrows show the number of vehicles. The point of the arrows show the direction the traffic was moving in. Flow line maps can also be used to show, for example, the movement of goods, or the movement of people.

FIGURE 4.23 *How to draw a simple flow line map*

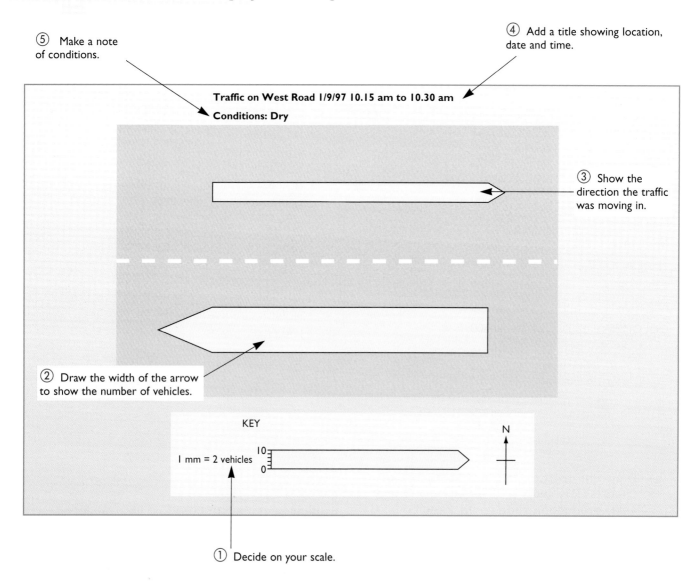

⑤ Make a note of conditions.

④ Add a title showing location, date and time.

Traffic on West Road 1/9/97 10.15 am to 10.30 am

Conditions: Dry

③ Show the direction the traffic was moving in.

② Draw the width of the arrow to show the number of vehicles.

KEY

1 mm = 2 vehicles

N

① Decide on your scale.

W O R K S H O P

1 Look at Figure 4.23. (a) How many vehicles went by in an easterly direction? (b) How many vehicles went by in a westerly direction?

FIGURE 4.24   *The UK's top three trading partners, 1994: statistics*

COUNTRY	EXPORTS (billions of pounds)	IMPORTS (billions of pounds)
Germany	18	21
United States	18	18
France	12	15

FIGURE 4.25   *The UK's top three trading partners, 1994: base map*

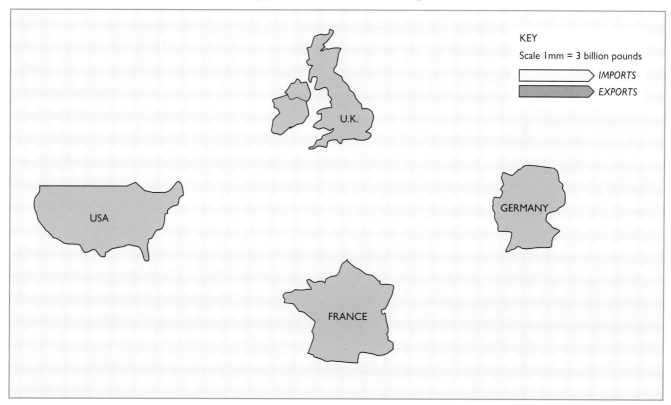

2 (You will need a copy of Figure 4.25 for this activity.) Use the statistics in Figure 4.24 to draw a flow line map to show the UK's **trade** with its 'top three' trading partners. The scale has been worked out for you.

3 What does your map tell you about the UK's trade?

W O R D   B O X

exports   goods or services sold to another country
imports   goods or services bought from another country
trade   the exchange of goods and services

Flow line maps 2

Introduction

Flow line maps can be drawn in a number of different ways. In Figure 4.26 a **banded scale**, rather than a **linear scale**, has been used. You cannot tell exactly how much traffic the flow lines stand for but you get a good idea of where the traffic is heaviest. The flow lines also follow the curve of the roads. Curved flow lines are quite difficult to draw. It is a good idea to use a flexible ruler.

FIGURE 4.26 *How to draw a banded flow line map*

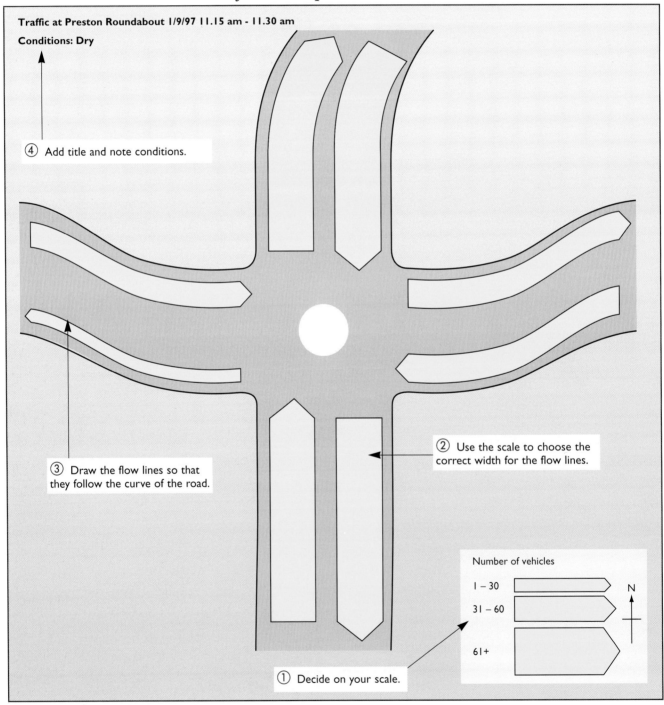

Traffic at Preston Roundabout 1/9/97 11.15 am - 11.30 am

Conditions: Dry

④ Add title and note conditions.

③ Draw the flow lines so that they follow the curve of the road.

② Use the scale to choose the correct width for the flow lines.

Number of vehicles

1 – 30

31 – 60

61+

N

① Decide on your scale.

1 (You will need a copy of Figure 4.28 for this activity.) Use the statistics in Figure 4.27 to draw a flow line map to show the pattern of **migration** to the UK in 1990. Sort the values into four equal 'bands'.

2 What does your map tell you about migration to the UK in 1990?

FIGURE 4.27   *Migration to the UK, 1990*

COUNTRIES	No. OF MIGRANTS (thousands)
EUROPEAN UNION	66
AUSTRALIA, NEW ZEALAND, CANADA	57
SOUTH ASIA (India, Bangladesh, Pakistan, Sri Lanka)	22
CARIBBEAN	7
USA	29
SOUTH AFRICA	6
MIDDLE EAST	10
OTHERS	70

FIGURE 4.28   *Flow line map: migration to the UK, 1990*

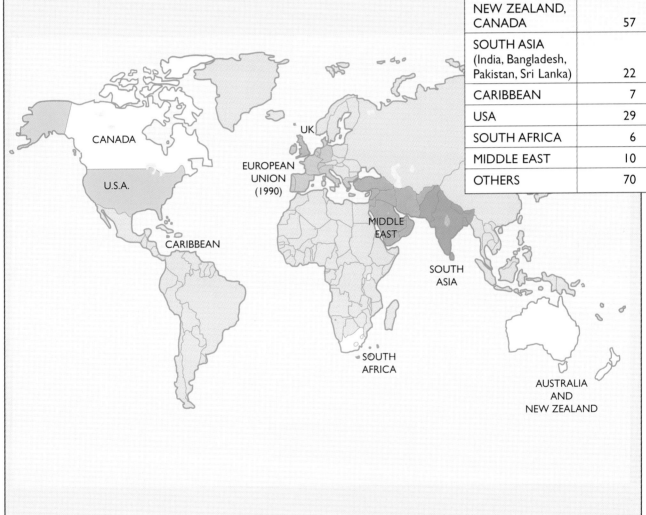

W O R D   B O X

banded scale   the values are organised into groups
linear scale   the values go up and down in order
migration   moving from one place to live in another

Flow line maps 3

Introduction

Flow lines can be divided up to show the **component parts** of a total. One way of doing this is to divide up the width using the flow line's scale. This is quite easy to work out but it can be difficult to draw. Figure 4.29 shows the component parts of the flow line on page 102.

FIGURE 4.29 *How to show the component parts of a flow line*

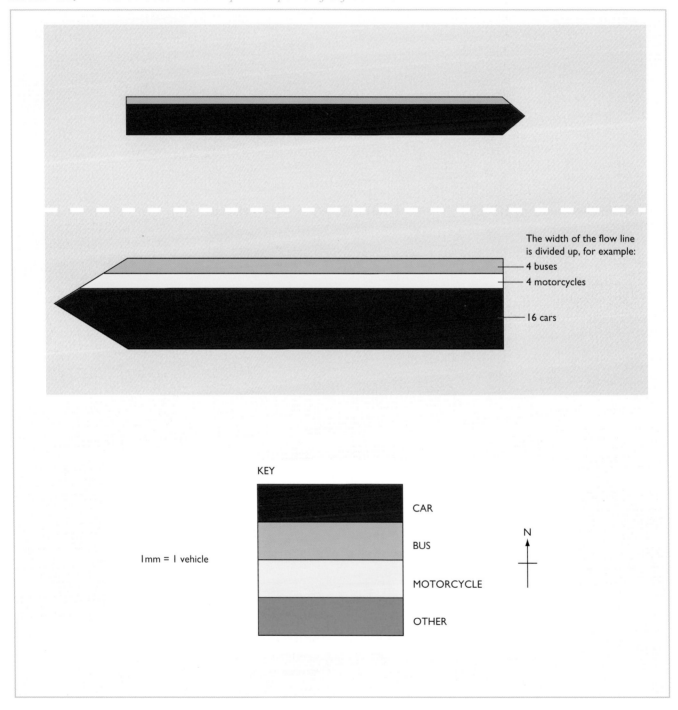

The width of the flow line is divided up, for example:
- 4 buses
- 4 motorcycles
- 16 cars

1mm = 1 vehicle

KEY

CAR
BUS
MOTORCYCLE
OTHER

N

1 What extra information does Figure 4.29 give us compared with the flow line on page 102?
2 (You will need a copy of Figure 4.31 for this activity.) Use the statistics in Figure 4.30 to draw a flow line map to show the movement of pedestrians in Huntingdon High Street. Use a **linear scale** (rather than a **banded scale**) and divide up the flow lines to show the number of men, women and children.
3 Describe the pattern your map shows.
4 What time of the day do you think the survey was carried out? Suggest a reason for your answer.
5 What problems do you think the students might have had collecting the data?

FIGURE 4.30 *Ten-minute pedestrian survey: Huntingdon High Street, 8.7.97*

LOCATION	MEN	WOMEN	CHILDREN
A	6	20	9
B	4	16	5
C	5	19	9
D	4	15	7
E	3	10	5
F	5	12	7
G	3	9	4
H	6	12	7

FIGURE 4.31 *Base map: Huntingdon High Street*

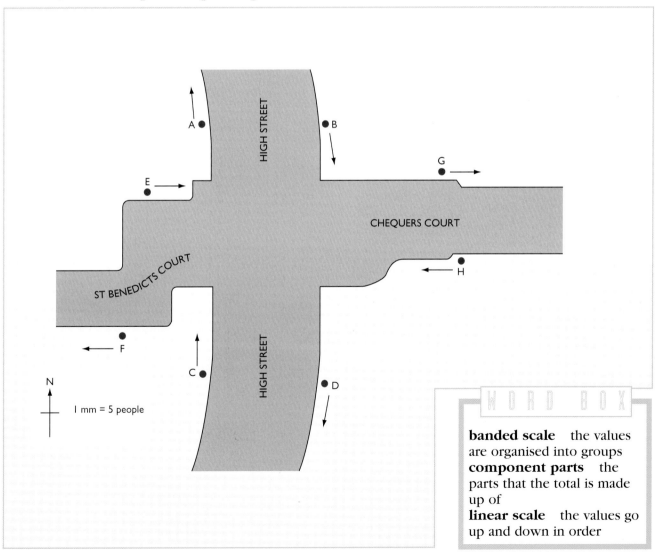

banded scale the values are organised into groups
component parts the parts that the total is made up of
linear scale the values go up and down in order

CHAPTER 5

Image Interpretation

5.1a *Sketching photographs*

Introduction

Photographs provide a useful record of a visit or image of a place. Drawing a labelled sketch of the photograph can help to highlight important features. Asking questions about the photograph can help recognise and discuss what is shown. For example, in Figure 5.1, what are those buildings used for? Who works here? Why was the factory built here? Or, how are goods moved to and from the factory?

FIGURE **5.1** *Sketch of Dema Glassworks*

Sketching photographs

It is not necessary to be a good artist to draw a sketch. There are some useful guidelines that can help to develop this skill. Figure 5.1 shows a way of drawing a sketch based on a photograph. A grid drawn on acetate or tracing paper could be placed over the photograph to act as a reference.

First, look carefully at the photograph. Are there any useful **landmarks** to base your sketch on, such as a large building or hill? Next, draw a broad outline. The landmarks will help you locate other smaller features. Once the skyline and landmarks have been drawn, add the finer detail, e.g. vegetation. Add labelled arrows to identify features that are partly hidden or difficult to draw. Finally, write a brief description about the location to go with your sketch.

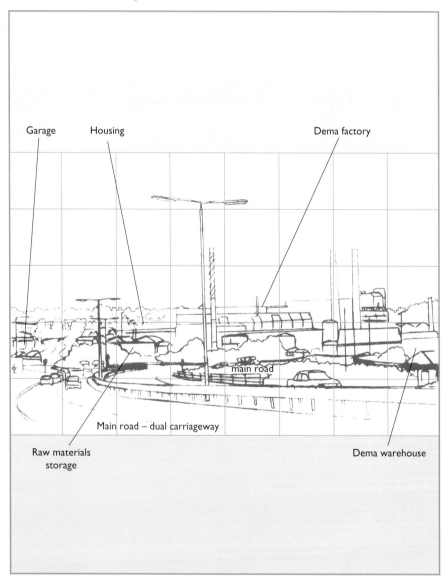

Garage   Housing   Dema factory

main road

Main road – dual carriageway

Raw materials storage

Dema warehouse

1 a) Draw an outline sketch of Figure 5.2.
  b) Label the following features: dual carriageway, roundabout, storage tanks, chimneys.
  c) Suggest four questions you would like to ask to find out about this factory.
2 Choose another photograph. Draw a simple labelled sketch and write a paragraph to describe your sketch.

FIGURE 5.2 *Dema Glassworks, Chesterfield, Derbyshire*

WORD BOX

landmark an important or easily recognisable feature

5.1b Sketching landscapes

Introduction

Figure 5.3 shows an industrial landscape, which has been **blighted**. Field sketching can be used to record geographical detail of a landscape. Photographs can be taken but a simple sketch can record specific observations, e.g. how industry has affected the landscape or reasons for location. A photograph can be used later to check with the field sketch.

FIGURE 5.3   *China Clay Pits, St. Austell, Cornwall*

Drawing a sketch

To draw a sketch first select a suitable vantage point that provides a clear view or use an appropriate photograph. Look at the skyline, then the middle ground and finally the foreground for detail (Figure 5.4). Decide on the extent of the view to be drawn. Draw on a feature either side to show the area to be sketched. Now draw a light vertical line through the centre and a horizontal line across the middle, following if possible an existing feature such as a road. The two lines will act as guidelines. Now draw on the skyline landmarks. Use these to fix the position of other features. This detail should be simple. Woodland can be drawn as curly lines, buildings as just roofs, or double lines to show roads. Once the field sketch is completed add notes and labels, e.g. land use or comments about specific features.

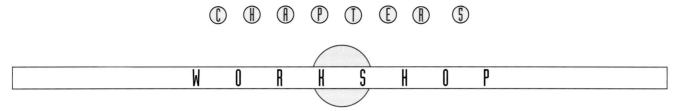

1 Figure 5.4 shows a partially completed sketch of the China Clay Pits.
Draw and complete your own copy of Figure 5.4.

FIGURE 5.4 *Sketch of China Clay Pits*

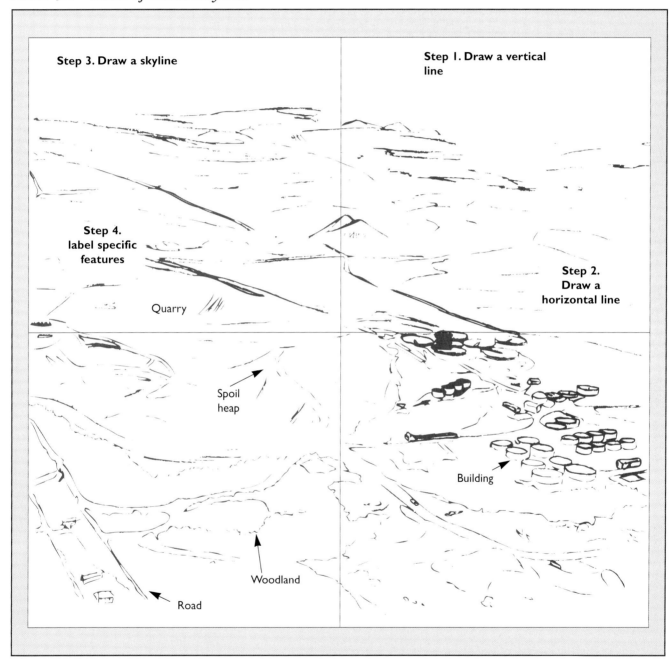

2 Field sketches can be used as a useful fieldwork technique. Use your
field sketching skills to investigate one of the following suggestions:
a view from your classroom window, a local factory or a physical
feature, or use your own ideas. On your field sketches add some
written notes to help you when drawing the neat copy.

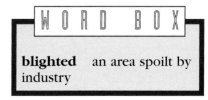

W O R D   B O X

blighted   an area spoilt by
industry

5.2a *Aerial photographs*

Introduction

Aerial photographs provide cartographers with an important and accurate source of geographical information. Many other people also use aerial photographs in their work, e.g. planners and archaeologists.

Taking aerial photographs

As an aircraft flies over the survey area it takes a series of overlapping **vertical** photographs with a mounted camera. The pictures are taken from the same height so they are all the same scale (Figure 5.5). An aerial survey would involve the aircraft flying over the area in a series of parallel runs. **Oblique** aerial photographs are taken at an angle and give a better idea of the landscape's height and features.

FIGURE **5.5** *Street map of area shown in figures 5.6 and 5.7*

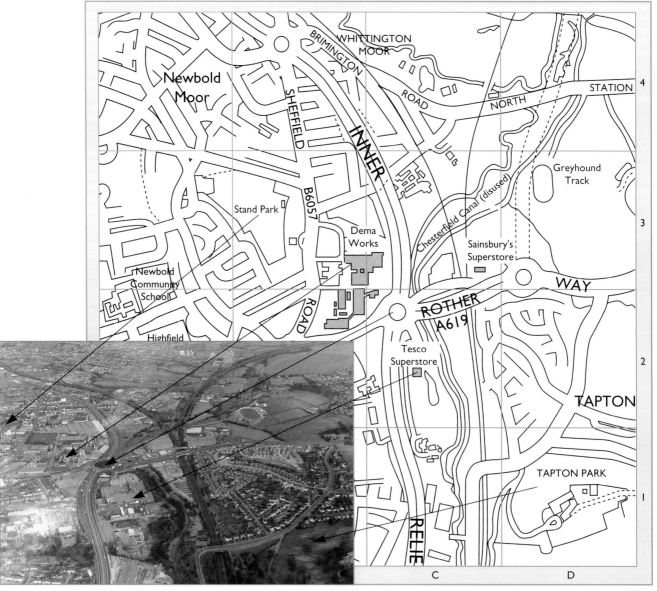

FIGURE **5.6** *Oblique photograph showing north of Chesterfield, Derbyshire*

W O R K S H O P

1 Look at Figure 5.7. Identify the features marked A–E on the photograph using the street map (Figure 5.5).
2 Draw an outline of Figure 5.7. Use the information from the map and photograph to:
  a) identify the names of the roads;
  b) colour in blue the Chesterfield Canal and the River Rother;
  c) colour in the main land use, industry, housing, the two superstores, derelict land and open space. Choose an appropriate colour for each land use. Add a key.

FIGURE 5.7   *Vertical photograph showing north of Chesterfield, Derbyshire*

5.2b Sketching aerial photographs

Introduction

By using the Basildon map extract with the photograph, it is possible to identify landmarks and land use patterns.

Identifying specific features

The areial photograph of Basildon (Figure 5.9), a wide north-south area along easting 70, shows a range of different land uses, both **rural** and **urban**. Specific features, such as the hospital, (grid reference 711872, square A1), the lake in Gloucester Park, (grid reference 711892, square A10), and the two roundabouts at grid reference 711884, square A7, can be used to locate the area shown on the map with the aerial photograph.

Identifying land use

Figure 5.8 shows a range of land use as sketch maps. The street layout provides a useful guide to drawing these maps.

WORD BOX

land use how the land is used, for example, farmland, golf course, or housing
rural countryside
urban built up area

Residential area with crescents e.g. grid reference 704 874

Farmland e.g. grid reference 708 871 – hedge field boundaries

Bus station e.g. grid reference 703 885 and railway line

Hospital buildings e.g. grid reference 701 872

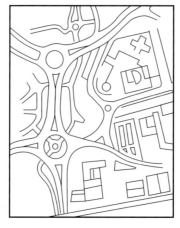

Roundabouts e.g. grid reference 701 884

FIGURE 5.8 *Sketches based on photographs*

1 Make a sketch of Figure 5.9. Draw a grid 5 by 10, number and lettered as Figure 5.9

2 Mark on the A1321, A176, the railway, the major roads, the central area of Basildon, (this is between the railway and A1321), the residential areas, the open space and label the golf course and Gloucester Park.

2 Add any details such as the hospital, the church, and the school, and complete a key.

FIGURE 5.9 *Aerial photograph of Basildon*

5.2c Matching maps to aerial photographs

Introduction

Maps are a simplified plan of an area. When used with a photograph the real detail, missing either because it is too small or difficult for a cartographer to show, can be identified. Matching photographs with maps goes beyond locating and identifying specific physical and human features. Archaeologists use aerial photographs with maps to recognise buried ruins or field systems. Development workers in LEDCs (Less Economically Developed Countries) use photographs with maps to locate water supplies or plan measures to reduce the effects of **desertification**.

The Millennium Dome

To help celebrate the **millennium**, industrial wasteland on the Greenwich **peninsula** is to be redeveloped. The centrepiece will be a dome. The proposed 5000 homes and commercial buildings will be an eco-friendly urban area. The ecologically sensitive flood protection scheme will provide a wildlife habitat (Figure 5.10).

Architects used photographs to complement the maps and illustrate the proposed plans. These show how the development will impact on the surrounding area.

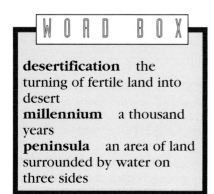

WORD BOX

desertification the turning of fertile land into desert
millennium a thousand years
peninsula an area of land surrounded by water on three sides

FIGURE 5.10 *Proposed development of the Greenwich Peninsula*

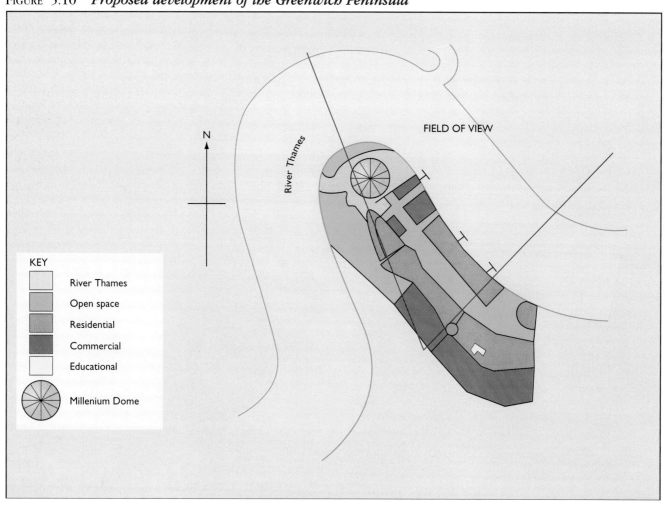

WORKSHOP

1 Describe the present land use shown in Figure 5.12.
2 Draw an outline of the Greenwich Peninsula based on Figure 5.12. Draw a sketch map to show the land use in Figure 5.10.
3 Use Figure 5.10 to describe the proposed land uses at zones A to D shown on Figure 5.11.
4 Draw a sketch based on Figures 5.10 and 5.11 to show the developments planned.

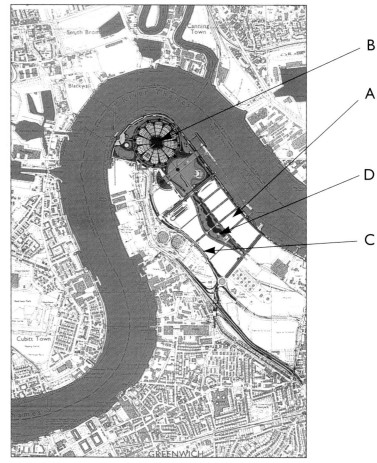

FIGURE 5.11 *Aerial view of the Greenwich Peninsula*

FIGURE 5.12 *Greenwich Peninsula looking east along the Thames*

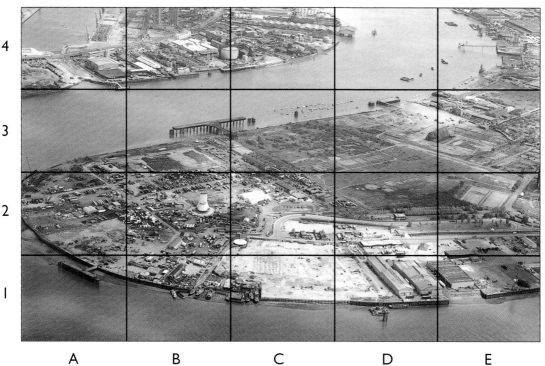

5.2d Weather maps and images

Introduction

Meteorologists provide accurate information about the weather. They use satellite images and computers to understand and predict the weather. This is essential information for many groups of people. Many economic activities rely on these forecasts, e.g. food chain stores plan which foods are most likely to sell, or, supply ships to North Sea oil rigs will only sail if the weather is fine. It is possible to use a fax to receive an up to date image from the Weather Centre at Bracknell.

Weather images

Satellites monitor global weather systems. The El Nino system has been responsible for storms, floods and drought in the tropical regions. It's origins in the Western Pacific Ocean have been traced by satellites. As the system spread eastwards towards the Americas its impact on sea temperatures and the weather has also been monitored.

Most of the British Isles' weather comes from the west. Satellite images provide detailed information about these systems. Figure 5.13 shows a severe storm over Europe. Satellites can track the storm and meteorologists are able to predict likely movement and possible weather forecasts.

FIGURE 5.13 *Photograph showing a storm over Europe*

Weather system

Meteorologists use synoptic charts to plot weather details (Figure 5.14). These maps use **isobars** to show the weather system. **Depressions** move eastwards, blown across the Atlantic Ocean by prevailing winds. The mix of warm, moist tropical air and cooler polar air produces cloud and rain along a front. As the depression moves across the country each sector brings its own set of weather. This helps explain why our weather is so changeable, but knowing the sequence helps the meteorologists predict conditions. In a high pressure system there is little or no cloud shown on a satellite image. The air is not being condensed by warmer or cooler air masses mixing with this stable air mass. The weather conditions are calm and skies clear. Compare the cloudy condition of Britain with the clearer conditions over Southern Fance.

FIGURE 5.14 *Weather map*

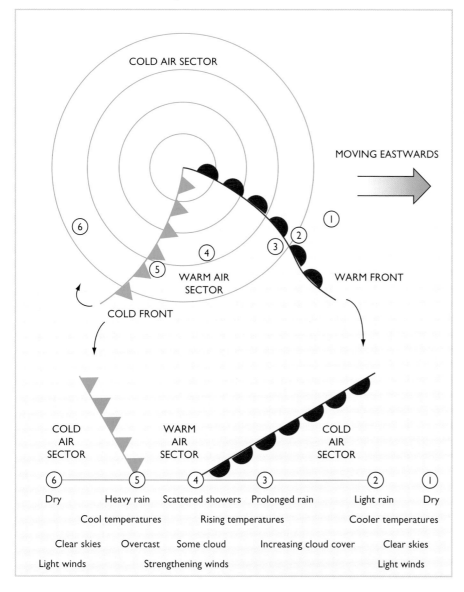

W O R K S H O P

1 Draw an outline of Figure 5.13: (a) trace the clouds; (b) add these labels: centre of the depression, warm front, cold front, warm air sector, cold air sector.
2 Assuming that the depression will move eastwards over the next 24 hours, describe the likely weather for East Anglia.
3 A **high pressure** is centred over much of Europe. How is this shown on a satellite image?
4 Explain how a satellite image can help meteorologists predict the weather.
5 Suggest why it may not always be possible to use a satellite image to help with forecasting.

W O R D   B O X

depression a low pressure system that brings wet and windy weather
high pressure a stable air mass that brings clear and calm conditions
isobars lines that join up places with equal air pressure
meteorologist a scientist who analyses and predicts the weather

5.3a *Satellite images*

Introduction

Satellite images taken from hundreds of miles away in space can provide information about a large area. Such images can identify settlements, natural features and land use.

Using satellite images

Satellites use different types of cameras to collect information. Some record visible light and provide a realistic photographic image, e.g. Figure 2.21. This shows the whole earth. It was taken by the Meteostat weather satellite. The realistic colouring was added by computer. Figure 5.16 shows a satellite image of Cumbria. The colours are natural. The image shows the region around the Lake District National Park.

Other cameras use infra-red light, which detects heat patterns. Figure 5.15 shows the infra-red satellite image of the city of Kobe, Japan. In the infra-red colour range, buildings appear light grey, vegetation appears in shades of red, water as blue/black, clouds are white. It is possible to see the dock area with several ships and new land created in the bay.

satellite image   a computer-enhanced picture taken from space

FIGURE 5.15   *Satellite image of Kobe Bay, Japan*

FIGURE 5.16   *Satellite photograph of Cumbria*

W O R K S H O P

1 Using an outline of Figure
5.16 and an atlas map of
north west England:
a) mark on the extent of
the Lake District, Forest
of Bowland and
Yorkshire Dales;
b) label Barrow,
Workington, Whitehaven,
Penrith and Kendal;
(c) identify each of the lakes
shown.

2 Figure 5.17 shows a
coloured Landstat image of
Montego Bay, western
Jamaica. Find Jamaica in an
atlas.
a) draw an outline of Figure
5.17;
b) locate Montego Bay on
your outline;
c) shade in the highland
area;
d) shade in the agricultural
lowlands;
e) locate the settlements.

3 On a copy of Figure 5.15
label these features:
airport, harbour area,
mountain areas, new land in
the bay, built up area of
Kobe, rivers.

Key

 highland

 agricultural land

 settlement

 sea

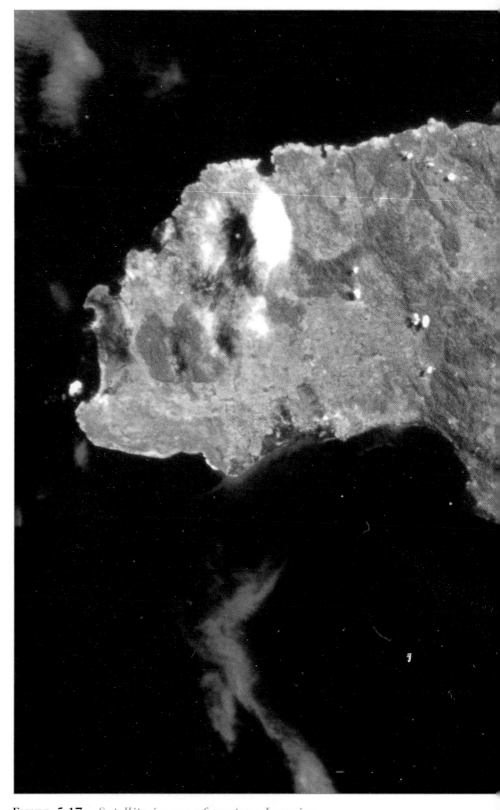

FIGURE 5.17 *Satellite image of western Jamaica*

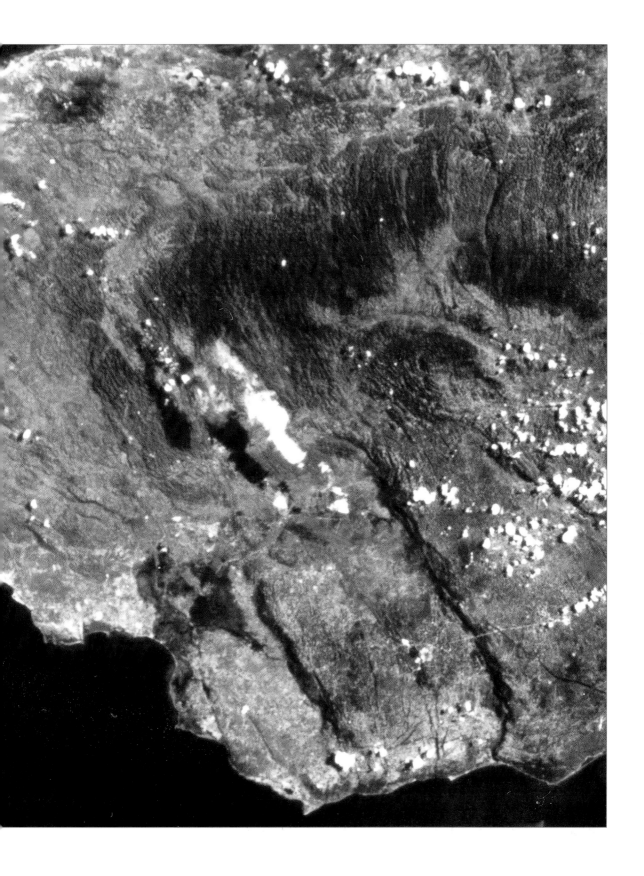

5.3b Identifying land use patterns

Introduction

Landscapes and land use patterns can be recognised from satellite images. Figure 5.18 shows part of the Saudi Arabian desert. The **prevailing wind** has created long sand ridges (called seif dunes). Figure 5.19 shows the El Fayyum Oasis, Egypt. The oasis is surrounded by the desert. The *irrigated* farmland is shown red and the Birkat Quarun Lake is black.

FIGURE 5.18 *Photograph of the Arabian desert*

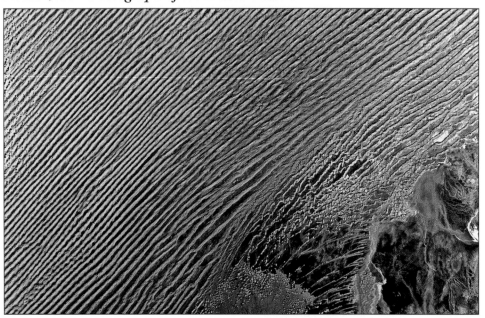

FIGURE 5.19 *Photograph of the El Fayyum Oasis, Egypt*

Identifying land use

Land use is often related to **relief**. Figure 5.20 shows how the flood plain of the River Barito, Kalimantan, Indonesia, has been cultivated. The **irrigation** canals mark out the square fields of the plantations. Not all of the flood plain has been cleared. The forest is being cleared by burning. In September 1997, these fires burnt out of control over a large area. The smoke caused pollution over a large area of south east Asia.

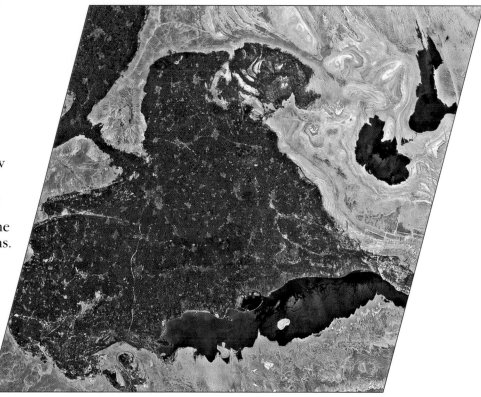

WORKSHOP

1 Draw an outline of Figure 5.18 to show the area of dunes and mountains.
2 On an outline of Figure 5.19: (a) colour the desert (yellow), lakes (blue), irrigated lands (green), and settlement (grey); (b) if the prevailing wind is northerly, shade as /// the areas likely to be threatened by encroaching sand dunes.
3 On an outline of Figure 5.20: (a) shade the forest; (b) draw on the field pattern; (c) indicate where the forest is being burnt.
4 Describe how the land changes from A to B.

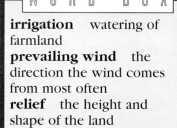

WORD BOX

irrigation   watering of farmland
prevailing wind   the direction the wind comes from most often
relief   the height and shape of the land

FIGURE 5.20   *Satellite image of the River Barito, Kalimantan, Indonesia*

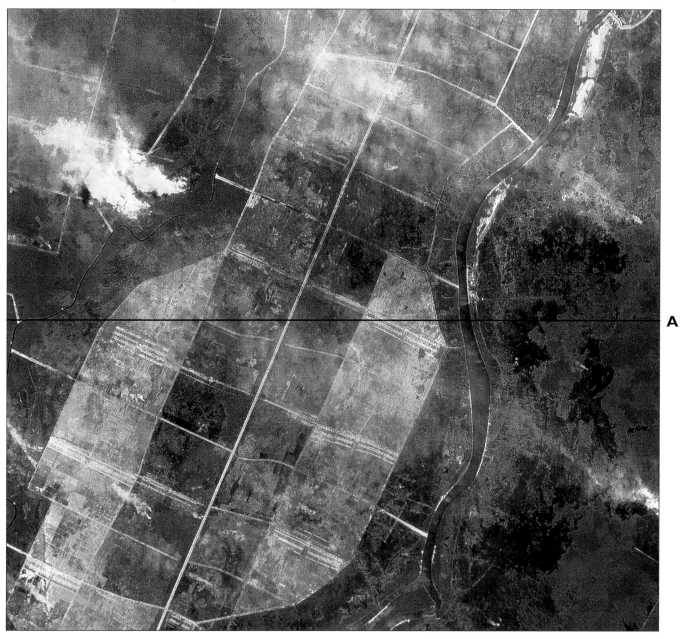

B   A

5.3c Analysing satellite images

Introduction

The earth is observed every second by the array of specialist satellites orbiting. Analysis of satellite images can provide information about natural phenomena and human activities. Computers are necessary to process the vast amount of information. **Trans-national corporations** involved in global food production use satellites to monitor potential crop yields and the impact of natural disasters on production. The information is used to plan cropping. Crop failure in the southern hemisphere can be balanced by an increase in planting elsewhere.

FIGURE 5.21 *Satellite image of rainforest destruction in Brazil*

E5	Untouched forest
C4	Roads
D1	Cultivated land

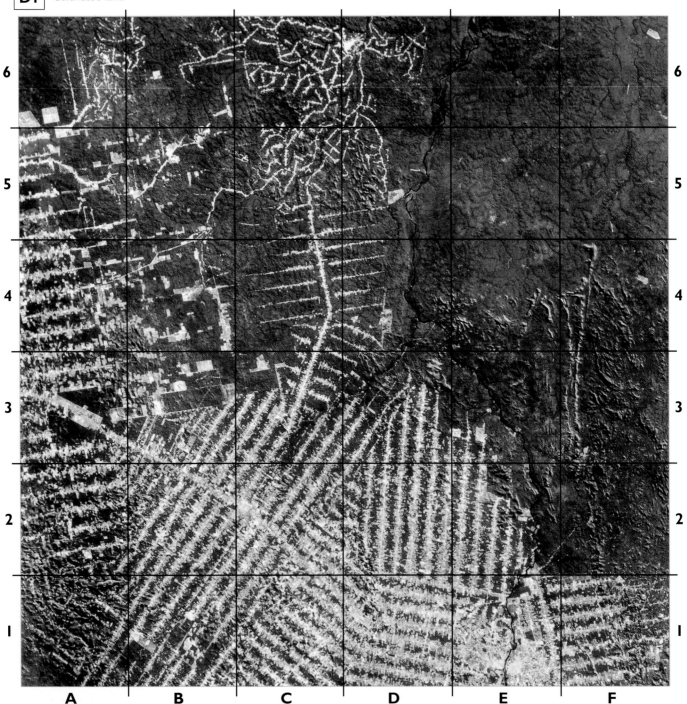

Using satellite photographs

The pressure for farmland and development affects the environment. Satellite images are used to monitor the damage caused by **deforestation**. Large scale deforestation in Brazil may cause changes to the global climate. The unique rainforest ecosystem will be destroyed and lost. Conservationists use a variety of satellite images to monitor and describe the deforestation. Monitoring by satellites shows the process of deforestation (Figure 5.21). Images can be used to show changes in an area over time. Figure 5.22 shows where slash and burn has cleared land for cattle ranching. The image is two frames taken a month apart then combined to show surface cover changes. The new grass growth is green, while the land burnt since is shown as red. Black shows previously cleared areas with no new growth. Figure 5.23 shows how the forest has been cleared as red patches of one square kilometre over a three-year period. The dark areas show previous deforestation.

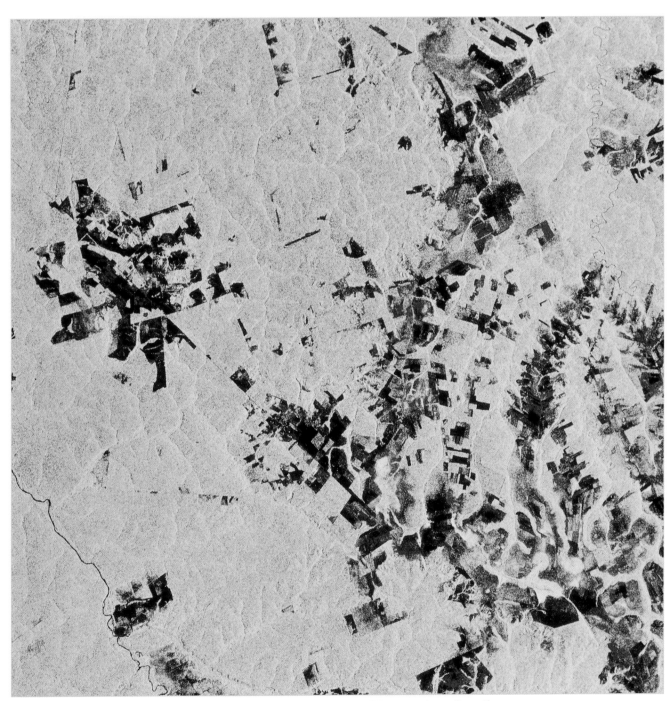

FIGURE 5.22 *Satellite image of rainforest destruction in Diamantina, Brazil*

W O R K S H O P

1 Study Figure 5.21.
   Find the grid squares A2 and B2. Look carefully at the pattern of roads and tracks.
   a) Draw the pattern shown in these squares.
   b) Describe how the forest has been cleared in each of these squares.

2 Find grid squares C5 and E1 in Figure 5.21.
   a) Draw the pattern shown in these squares.
   b) Describe how the forest has been cleared in each of these squares.

3 Using Figure 5.22:
   a) trace an overlay map to show: (i) new forest clearance – shown as red; (ii) other forest clearance – shown as black and green; (iii) unaffected land – yellow.
   b) Describe where the new forest clearance has occurred.
   c) On your overlay suggest likely places where future clearance will take place.

4 Calculate the percentage of land use on Figure 5.23:
   a) Draw a grid 10 × 10 squares to cover Figure 5.23. One square equals one per cent.
   b) Lay the grid over the photograph. For each square, decide whether the land has been: (i) cleared since 1986; (ii) cleared before 1986; (iii) unaffected.
   c) Present your findings as a graph adding a description.

5 Explain how satellite images help conservationists monitor deforestation and other environmental issues.

WORD BOX

deforestation   clearance of forest for development and farming
trans-national corporations   (or multi-nationals), large companies with operations in more than one country

FIGURE **5.23**   *Satellite image of rainforest deforestation in Aldeia Velha, Brazil*

CHAPTER 6
Using Information Technology

6.1 *Using Information Technology (IT)*

Introduction

IT has many uses in geography. These two pages will help you to make the most of IT in school and as part of coursework/fieldwork. Figure 6.1 lists some of the main uses of IT. Figure 6.2 gives some of the main reasons for using IT. Figure 6.3 shows some of the IT resources that you could use. There are other things you could use as well. For example, there are digital cameras and Geographical Information Systems (GIS) that combine maps with huge databases of statistics and photographs.

FIGURE 6.1 **What can you use IT for?**

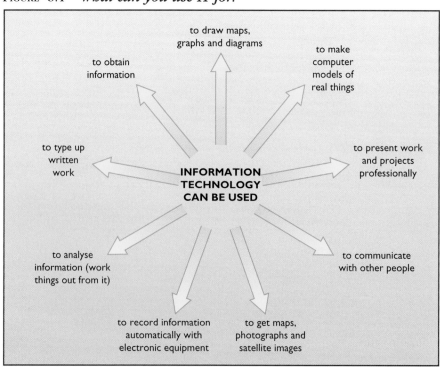

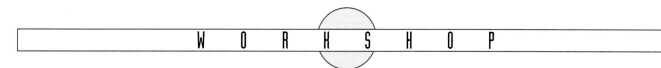

W O R K S H O P

1 Make a list of the things you have used IT for in geography already.
2 What, if any, IT resources do you have: (a) at home; (b) at school in the geography classroom/area; (c) at school in the library/Resources Centre; (d) in your local library; (e) in the main library.
3 Think back over the work you have done in geography during the last six months. Write about two things that you could have used IT for.
4 Write about two things that you would like to use IT for in the next six months.

FIGURE 6.2 *Why use IT?*

- **It helps you to do some things much more quickly, e.g. drawing a graph. This gives you more time to think about the geography.**

- **It is easy to change things on a computer, so drafting and re-drafting, and experimenting with different types of graph, for example, becomes possible.**

- **It allows you to handle an enormous amount of data so that you can answer more questions, more fully.**

- **It can make some things, such as shading in a map, much easier.**

- **It lets you do many things that simply are not possible without a computer, e.g. using the Internet.**

FIGURE 6.3 *IT word box*

WHAT?	WHAT FOR?	EXAMPLE
database	recording, analysing and presenting data (words and numbers)	a database of development indicators
spreadsheet	recording mainly numbers in a table, carrying out calculations and presenting data	working out the population of a country in 50 years time
word processor	writing text	typing a report about an earthquake
Desk Top Publishing package	putting together text, maps, graphs, photographs etc as a finished piece of work	presenting an account of an oil spill with a map and photographs as well as a typed report
'Draw' programme	drawing maps and diagrams; adding to / changing maps, diagrams and photographs	drawing a flow diagram of the hydrological cycle; using graded shading to show levels of unemployment in different countries
CD-ROM	finding out information from a computerised encyclopaedia, large database, collection of photographs etc.	playing a geographical game about the growth and development of a city
Internet	searching for information on the World Wide Web	searching for up to date information about rainforest destruction
E-mail	swapping messages and data with other people anywhere in the world	swapping weather data with schools in other countries
data logger	automatically collecting data	collecting soil and air temperature for a 24 hour period

6.2 *Databases*

Databases 1

Introduction

A database is used to record information. It is a very useful tool for a number of reasons:

● you can find and sort out information quickly;

● it analyses data for you, e.g. it will work out averages; and

● it helps you to present information in a number of different ways, e.g. as graphs.

There are many different database programs but they all work in much the same way. Each set of data is known as a **record**. Each piece of information is known as a **field**. For example, Figure 6.4 is a record made up of eight fields.

FIGURE 6.4 *An example of a record with eight fields*

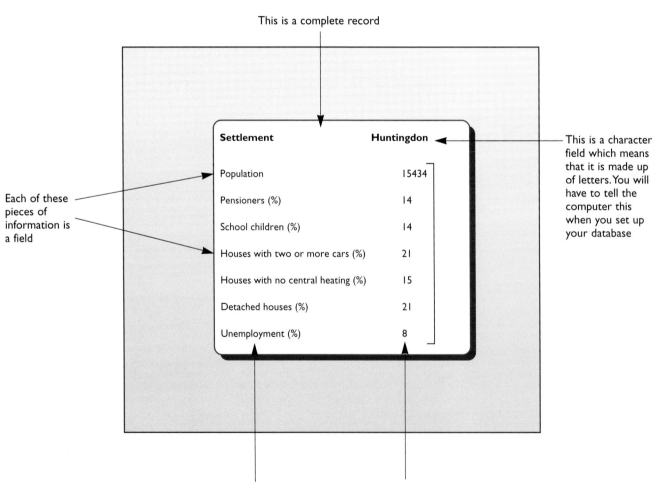

This is a complete record

Settlement	Huntingdon
Population	15434
Pensioners (%)	14
School children (%)	14
Houses with two or more cars (%)	21
Houses with no central heating (%)	15
Detached houses (%)	21
Unemployment (%)	8

Each of these pieces of information is a field

This is a character field which means that it is made up of letters. You will have to tell the computer this when you set up your database

These fields are all too long to fit into a database, so you will have to use short names instead

These fields are all numeric which means that they are made up of numbers. Again, you will have to tell the computer this when you set up your database

1 Set up a database for the records shown in Figure 6.5. You will need to follow the instructions for your type of database and you will need to follow these steps.
   Step 1: Set up a blank record. This should have all eight fields on it. You may have to use the short names. Remember to choose the right type of field: character (letters) or numeric (numbers).
   Step 2: Save this record and give your database a name.
   Step 3: Enter the data for all of the records. Save every time you finish a record so that there is less chance of losing information if something goes wrong.

2 Use the different functions of the database to answer the following questions:
   a) Sort the settlements into order of population, highest first.
   b) Find out the names of settlements with more than 12 per cent of pensioners.
   c) Find out the names of the settlements where the percentage of houses with two or more cars is greater than 40%.
   d) Use the statistics function to find the mean (average) figure (%) for: (i) school children; (ii) houses with no central heating; and (iii) detached houses.
   e) Draw a bar chart to show the percentage of unemployed people.

W O R D   B O X
field   a piece of information
record   a set of data

FIGURE 6.5   *Population database: Huntingdon area, 1991*

Sett	**Godmanchester**
Pop	5389
Pension	15
SchChi	29
Twocars	14
NoCH	11
DetHou	30
Unempl	5

Sett	**Stukeleys**
Pop	2056
Pension	8
SchChi	13
Twocars	45
NoCH	3
DetHou	40
Unempl	2

Sett	**Southoe**
Pop	465
Pension	12
SchChi	20
Twocars	53
NoCH	12
DetHou	76
Unempl	7

Sett	**Little Paxton**
Pop	3195
Pension	12
SchChi	16
Twocars	41
NoCH	5
DetHou	28
Unempl	6

Sett	**Spaldwick**
Pop	304
Pension	19
SchChi	15
Twocars	50
NoCH	18
DetHou	47
Unempl	5

Sett	**St Neots**
Pop	25116
Pension	13
SchChi	14
Twocars	30
NoCH	8
DetHou	25
Unempl	7

Sett	**Grafham**
Pop	452
Pension	8
SchChi	15
Twocars	61
NoCH	5
DetHou	70
Unempl	4

Sett	**St Ives**
Pop	15314
Pension	13
SchChi	15
Twocars	32
NoCH	12
DetHou	29
Unempl	5

Sett	**Ellington**
Pop	623
Pension	20
SchChi	18
Twocars	53
NoCH	7
DetHou	73
Unempl	4

Databases 2

Introduction

Setting up your own database is quite straightforward, but you have to go through a number of stages very carefully (Figure 6.6).

The first question you have to ask yourself is 'Should I be using a database?'. If you want to sort out certain facts from large amounts of data, e.g. all of the earthquakes greater than 7 on the Richter scale since 1970, or all of the settlements in the UK with a population of more than 1 million, as well as present and analyse that information, then the answer is 'yes'. However, if you only want to present the information and/or to analyse it, another tool, such as a graphics package or a spreadsheet, might be better.

The next stage is to plan the database with pencil and paper – it will save time in the long run! What fields are you going to include? Is the data in the form of numbers or letters? How do you want the display to look? You may have to give 'short names' for the fields: do these names make sense? Is the information available for all records?

You are now ready to set up a blank record. Save it and give the database a name. Enter data for the first four or five records, save it and try it out. Does it work as you had intended, or are some of the fields unnecessary? Do the 'short names' need changing? It is very unusual to get a database right first time, but trying it out means that you can change it before you have spent hours inputting data.

When the database is how you want it to be, enter the data for all of the records. Save regularly so that the chances of losing data are slight: typing errors and other mistakes are easy to change.

Your database is now ready to use. If it is a good database it will allow you to do a large number of things that would take ages to do 'long hand'. However, you still have to be a geographer to get the most out of it so do not forget important geographical questions such as Where is it? What is it like? How did it get like that? How is it changing? What will it be like in the future?

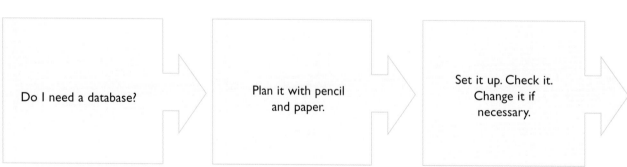

Do I need a database? → Plan it with pencil and paper. → Set it up. Check it. Change it if necessary. →

FIGURE 6.6 *Setting up a database*

W O R K S H O P

1 Set up a database of social and economic **indicators** for 25 countries. An atlas and/or a digest of geographical statistics are likely to be good sources of information.

- Ten of the countries should be **MEDCs** and 15 of the countries should be **LEDCs**. Use the **North–South Development Line** to separate MEDCs from LEDCs.
- Each record should have nine fields - one of these will be the name of the country and one will be whether it is an MEDC or LEDC but you must choose and research the other seven fields (indicators).

2 When you have set up your database and entered all of the information, print out one of the records.

3 Try out all of the functions of your database.

4 Use the graph and/or statistics function to draw scatter graphs to see if there is a relationship (correlation) between any of the indicators (see pages 24–25). If you do find a correlation, try to explain it.

5 Write an account of your database project:

- Describe what you were asked to do.
- On an outline map of the world, mark on and label your 25 countries.
- Explain why you chose your indicators. Did they turn out to be good indicators?
- Write down at least ten things you have learnt from your database.
- Include any graphs that you have drawn. Add labels to explain what they show.
- Write a short evaluation of the project. Did you enjoy it? Give reasons.

Enter the data.
Save regularly.
Check the entries.

Use it to answer important geographical questions, e.g.
Where is it?
What is it like?
How did it get like that?
How is it changing?
What will it be like in the future?

6.3 *Word processing and Desk Top Publishing*

Introduction

A word processor is more than just an electronic typewriter. As well as correcting mistakes, adding and deleting sentences and changing the size and type (**font**) of the letters you will be able to do many, if not all, of the following:

- check spellings;
- check grammar;
- use a **thesaurus**;
- add pictures, graphs and diagrams;
- number pages;
- add footnotes.

Word processing is particularly useful in geography for writing up projects. It means that you can make changes easily, e.g. if you have written a first draft for checking by your teacher. It is easy to change figure numbers. You can check the spelling and grammar. You can print it out with a 'professional look'. Even if you are a slow typist, word processing an important project is well worth it.

A Desk Top Publishing (DTP) package lets you put together text, pictures, maps, graphs and diagrams exactly as if it was a real newspaper, magazine or book. For example, it puts your text into columns and it makes text go round pictures.

There are many different DTP packages. Some are used by publishers while others are simpler but are still perfectly acceptable for presenting a project. Many word processing packages do almost as much as a DTP package, e.g. letting you write in columns and making text go round pictures.

It could be worth using a DTP package for that really special report, but it is a good idea to try it out first on a much shorter piece of work.

WORD BOX

font   style of letter
thesaurus   this gives lists of words that mean the same as each other, or are similar to each other

WORKSHOP

This activity asks you to try out some of the main word processing and DTP skills. All packages work in much the same way but to find out exactly how to do something you will have to read the instructions for your software.

1. Find out about a volcanic eruption. You will need to know where and when it happened, why it happened, what damage it caused, how people coped with the disaster, and what the future holds.
2. Word process the text of your report. Check the spellings (and grammar if you can) and make sure it covers all the points you have been asked to research.
3. Set out your report using a DTP package, making sure that you do all the things described in Figure 6.7.
4. Save your report onto a disc and then print it out.

FIGURE 6.7 *Desk Top Publishing your volcanoes report*

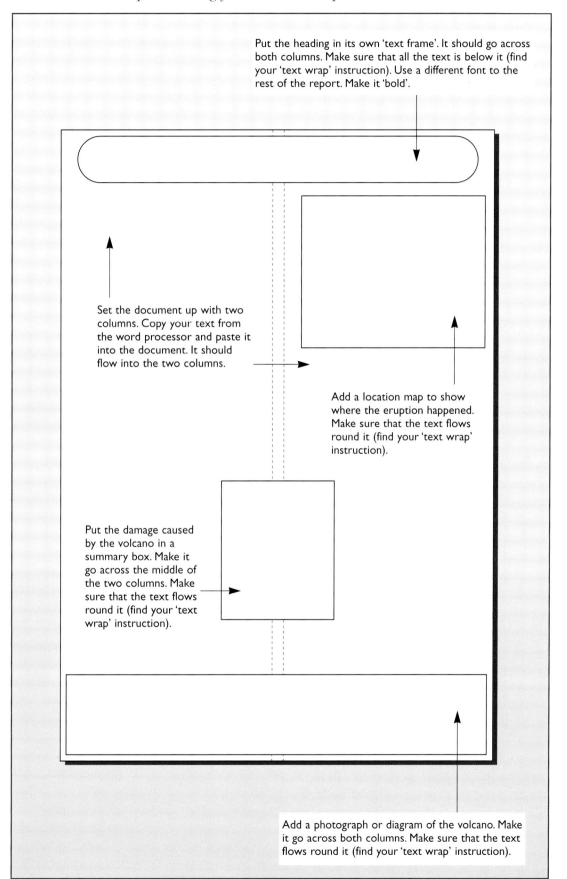

Put the heading in its own 'text frame'. It should go across both columns. Make sure that all the text is below it (find your 'text wrap' instruction). Use a different font to the rest of the report. Make it 'bold'.

Set the document up with two columns. Copy your text from the word processor and paste it into the document. It should flow into the two columns.

Add a location map to show where the eruption happened. Make sure that the text flows round it (find your 'text wrap' instruction).

Put the damage caused by the volcano in a summary box. Make it go across the middle of the two columns. Make sure that the text flows round it (find your 'text wrap' instruction).

Add a photograph or diagram of the volcano. Make it go across both columns. Make sure that the text flows round it (find your 'text wrap' instruction).

6.4 *Spreadsheets*

Spreadsheets 1

Introduction

A spreadsheet can be used to record any geographical information that can be set out as a table. Each box in the spreadsheet is known as a **cell**. You can type words and numbers in the cells and then use the spreadsheet to draw graphs. You can also type **formulae** into the cells and use the spreadsheet to carry out calculations.

There are many different spreadsheets programs, but they all work in much the same way. The main features of a spreadsheet are shown in Figure 6.8.

FIGURE 6.8 *An example of a blank spreadsheet*

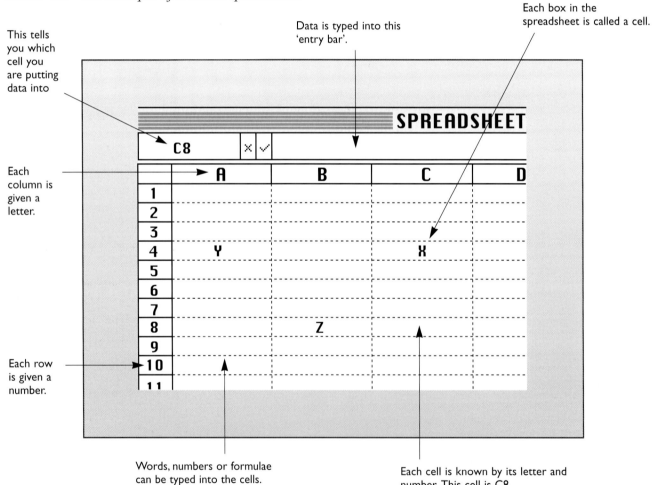

This tells you which cell you are putting data into

Data is typed into this 'entry bar'.

Each box in the spreadsheet is called a cell.

Each column is given a letter.

Each row is given a number.

Words, numbers or formulae can be typed into the cells.

Each cell is known by its letter and number. This cell is C8.

W O R K S H O P

1 Look at Figure 6.8. Write down the **co-ordinates** of cells X, Y and Z.
2 a) Figure 6.9 shows a spreadsheet set up with the populations of the countries in the European Union. Follow the instructions for the spreadsheet on your computer and set up a spreadsheet like this one.
   b) Use your spreadsheet to draw a bar chart of these figures.
   c) Use your spreadsheet to draw a pie chart of these figures.
   d) Cell B15 has worked out the total population of the countries of the European Union. Change the figure for the United Kingdom in cell B1 to 100. What has happened to the total population figure in cell B15?
   e) Can you find figures that are more up to date than 1993? If you can, you could enter them into the spreadsheet and the total would be automatically updated. You could redraw your graphs in a few seconds as well!

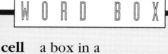

W O R D   B O X

cell   a box in a spreadsheet into which you can type words, numbers or formulae
co-ordinates   a way of identifying a square
formulae   a set of mathematical symbols for carrying out a calculation

FIGURE 6.9   *European Union population spreadsheet*

EU POPULATION

| B15 | × ✓ | =SUM(B1..B14) |

	A	B	C	D
1	UK	58		
2	Ireland	4		
3	Denmark	5		
4	Greece	11		
5	Italy	57		
6	France	58		
7	Netherlands	15		
8	Belgium/Luxembourg	11		
9	Germany	82		
10	Spain	40		
11	Portugal	11		
12	Austria	8		
13	Sweden	9		
14	Finland	5		
15	Total (millions)	374		
16				

The formula to add up the total population of the countries has been typed into cell B15. Different spreadsheets use different formulae, so check your instructions.

Spreadsheets 2

Introduction

Spreadsheets are an excellent way to record, analyse and present many types of **primary data**. You could try out this example for yourself, or you could read about it to get some ideas for your own projects.

W O R K S H O P

An investigation into environmental quality

(a)   Aim: To test the **hypothesis** that the quality of the **built environment** changes as you move away from the centre of a town.

(b)   Method:

    i)   On a map draw a **transect** from the centre of the town to its outskirts.

    ii)   At every twentieth building carry out an Environmental Quality Analysis (EQA) using the scoring system in Figure 6.10. Record your results as a table in the same form as the spreadsheet in Figure 6.11.

FIGURE 6.10   *Scoring system for Environmental Quality Analysis (EQA)*

Give each location a score out of five against the following categories

BUILDING CONDITION	STREET CONDITION	NOISE	LITTER	GENERAL APPEARANCE
5 = very good condition	5 = pavements and road are in very good condition	5 = very quiet	5 = hardly any litter at all	5 = very pleasant, eg trees and plenty of space
4	4	4	4	4
3 = satisfactory condition	3 = they are in satisfactory condition	3 = quite noisy	3 = some litter	3 = quite pleasant
2	2	2	2	2
1 = very poor condition	1 = they are in very poor condition	1 = very noisy	1 = a lot of litter	1 = not very pleasant at all eg no greenery, no space

(c) Analysis, presentation and explanation:
  i) Set up a spreadsheet like the one in Figure 6.11 and enter your fieldwork data.
  ii) Choose an appropriate type of graph to present the results for each location (row). Your graphs could be displayed on a base map. Describe and explain any pattern your map shows.
  iii) Choose an appropriate type of graph to present the results for each category (columns). Describe and explain what your graph shows.
  iv) Set up the final column to calculate the total score for each location. Use these figures as the basis for a graded shading map, one square per building (see pages 90–93). Describe and explain any pattern your map shows.
  v) Set up the final row to calculate the average score for each category. Use this information to check for locations that were a lot above or a lot below the average. Try to explain your results.

FIGURE 6.11 *EQA spreadsheet*

built environment the features of the landscape that have been made by people
hypothesis an idea to be tested
primary data information that you have collected from your own fieldwork observations, e.g. a traffic count
transect a route along which observations are recorded

The rows are used for the locations (the places where the survey was carried out).

The columns are used for categories.

G4

	A	B	C	D	E	F	G
1		Building	Street	Noise	Litter	Appearance	Total
2	Location 1	4	4	5	4	5	22
3	Location 2	2	3	1	2	2	10
4	Location 3	2					
5	Location 4	2					
6	Location 5	5					
7	Location 6	5					
8	Location 7	5					
9	Average	3.57					
10							
11							

You will be able to survey many more than 7 locations!

The cells in row 9 are used to calculate the average score for the category, rounded to two decimal places. The formula for this spreadsheet for this cell (check your instructions) was =ROUND(AVERAGE(B2..B8);2).

The cells in this column are used to calculate the total score for the location. The formula for this spreadsheet for this cell (check your instructions) was =SUM(B3..F3).

Using a spreadsheet means that working out averages and totals can be done very quickly. You will also be able to draw graphs of the data you have collected.

Evaluation:
  i) What problems did you have carrying out the survey?
  ii) Are there any ways in which your results might be misleading or inaccurate?
  iii) How could the project be improved and/or developed?
Conclusions:
  i) Give a brief summary of the main things that you have discovered.
  ii) Was your hypothesis true?

6.5 *Draw and paint programs*

Draw 1

Introduction

Draw and Paint programs are very useful in geography for drawing maps and diagrams. There are many different types of Draw and Paint programs but they all work in much the same way. Figure 6.12 shows how a Draw program can be used to present a flow diagram. Figure 6.13 shows how a Draw program can be used to label a map.

FIGURE 6.12 *Drawing a flow diagram: the erosion of a headland*

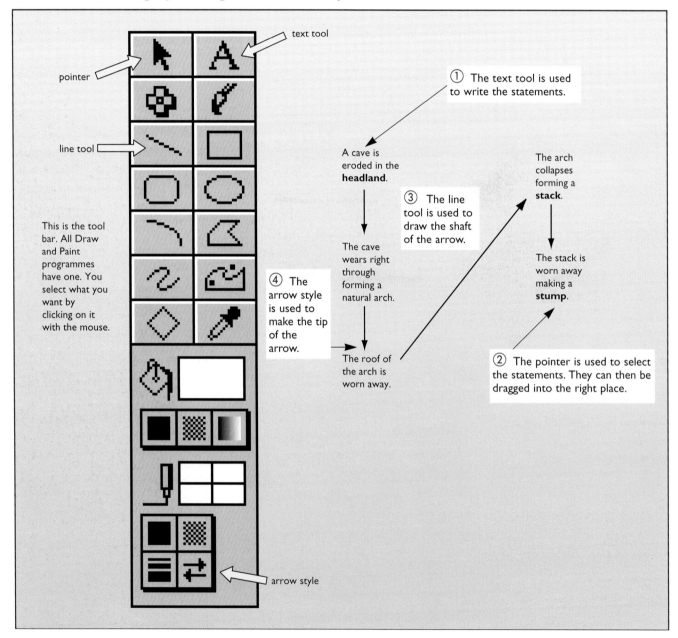

FIGURE 6.13   *Labelling a map: Australia's state capitals*

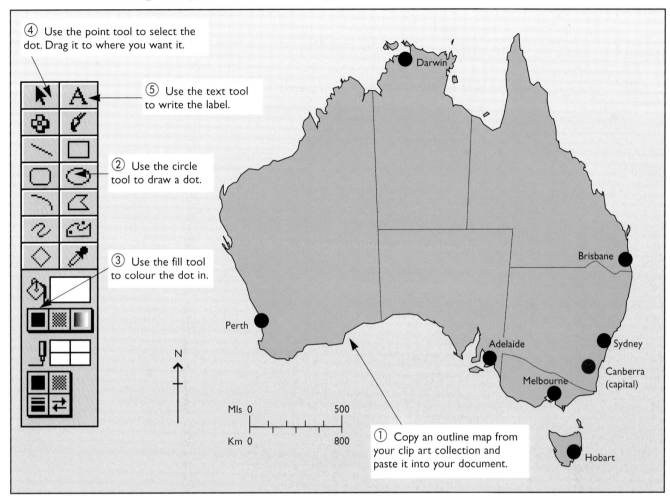

④ Use the point tool to select the dot. Drag it to where you want it.

⑤ Use the text tool to write the label.

② Use the circle tool to draw a dot.

③ Use the fill tool to colour the dot in.

Darwin

Brisbane

Perth

N

Adelaide

Sydney

Canberra (capital)

Melbourne

Mls 0   500
Km 0   800

① Copy an outline map from your clip art collection and paste it into your document.

Hobart

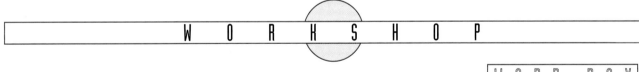

W O R K S H O P

1 Use your Draw program to draw a flow diagram of these statements about the **hydrological cycle**. You will have to sort them out into the right order.
   ● the clouds are blown over the land
   ● water **evaporates** from the sea
   ● the rivers take the water back to the sea
   ● water vapour **condenses** to form clouds
   ● the rain finds its way into rivers
   ● rain falls over the land

2 Use your Draw program to draw a map to show these UK towns and cities: London, Birmingham, Manchester, Liverpool, Leeds, Sheffield, Glasgow, Edinburgh, Newcastle-upon-Tyne, Bristol, Belfast, Nottingham, Norwich, Cardiff.

W O R D   B O X

condenses   changes from a gas to a liquid (water vapour to water droplets)
evaporates   changes from a liquid to a gas (water to water vapour)
headland   a band of rock jutting out into the sea
hydrological cycle   the water cycle
stack   a pillar of rock surrounded by the sea
stump   a lump of rock covered by the sea at high tide

Draw 2

Introduction

'Draw and Paint' programs can be used to draw more complicated types of maps and diagrams. The results look very professional and, because you can save them on the computer, they are easy to redraw. Figures 6.14 and 6.15 are two examples.

FIGURE 6.14   *Drawing a flow line map: Spain, origin of tourists, 1990*

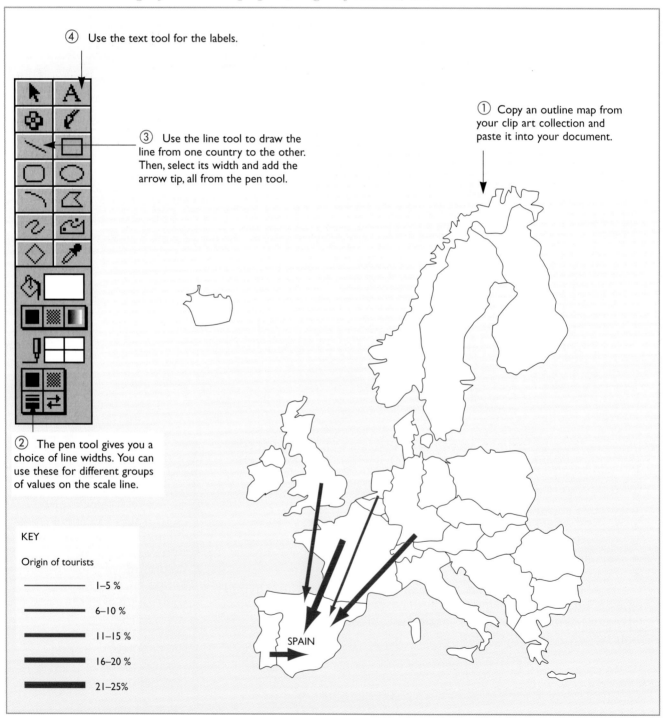

④ Use the text tool for the labels.

③ Use the line tool to draw the line from one country to the other. Then, select its width and add the arrow tip, all from the pen tool.

① Copy an outline map from your clip art collection and paste it into your document.

② The pen tool gives you a choice of line widths. You can use these for different groups of values on the scale line.

KEY

Origin of tourists

———— 1–5 %

———— 6–10 %

———— 11–15 %

———— 16–20 %

———— 21–25%

SPAIN

FIGURE 6.15 *Drawing a graded shading map: population density in the European Union*

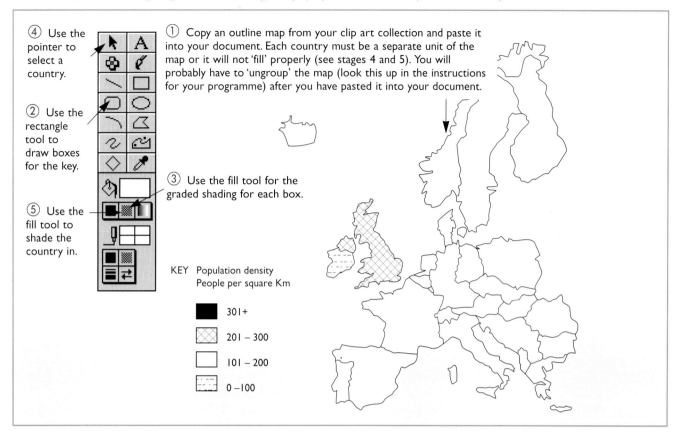

④ Use the pointer to select a country.

② Use the rectangle tool to draw boxes for the key.

⑤ Use the fill tool to shade the country in.

① Copy an outline map from your clip art collection and paste it into your document. Each country must be a separate unit of the map or it will not 'fill' properly (see stages 4 and 5). You will probably have to 'ungroup' the map (look this up in the instructions for your programme) after you have pasted it into your document.

③ Use the fill tool for the graded shading for each box.

KEY Population density People per square Km

■ 301+

▨ 201 – 300

□ 101 – 200

▤ 0 –100

WORKSHOP

1 Use your Draw program to draw a flow line map to show the **origin** of tourists to Greece (1990): Germany 21 per cent; UK 20 per cent; Italy 7 per cent; France 6 per cent; Yugoslavia 5 per cent. You can use the same key as the one in Figure 6.14.

2 Use your Draw program to draw a graded shading map to show **population density** in the European Union. The statistics that you need are given in Figure 6.16. You can use the same key as the one in Figure 6.15 where the first three countries have been completed as examples.

3 Describe and suggest reasons for the pattern your map shows.

WORD BOX

origin   where something comes from
population density   the number of people living in a given area, e.g. one square kilometre

FIGURE 6.16 *Population density in the European Union, 1995 (people per square kilometre)*

COUNTRY	POPULATION DENSITY
UK	241
Netherlands	457
Ireland	52
Germany	235
France	106
Austria	97
Spain	79
Finland	17
Portugal	115
Sweden	2
Belgium	309
Denmark	122
Luxembourg	153
Greece	82
Italy	194

6.6 *CD ROMs*

Introduction

CD ROM stands for 'Compact Disc – Read Only Memory'. CD ROMs store large amounts of information that can be understood by a computer. They are used for many things, for example:

- multimedia games;
- encyclopaedias;
- databases;
- atlases;
- picture libraries.

Many of you will use a CD ROM encyclopaedia when you are given a project to do in geography. In many respects they are more interesting than an ordinary encyclopaedia because you may be able to view moving images (e.g. of a volcanic eruption) and hear sound recordings (e.g. of a country's traditional music), as well as view maps and pictures, and read text. They are also easy to search through: tell the computer to find a particular topic and it will do it for you, without you having to find the right pages in the right book of a twenty volume encyclopaedia. Another advantage is that many CD ROMs are updated every year.

However, there is one thing that you should definitely not do: DO NOT COPY SECTIONS OF THE TEXT FROM THE CD ROM AND PASTE THEM STRAIGHT INTO YOUR WORK. You must show that you have read through the information, thought about it and understood it. This means 'putting it into your own words' and the only really successful way of doing this is to have some 'geographical questions' to answer (see the activity on the next page).

You must also 'quote your source', which means that you must write down the name of the encyclopaedia. You should also check the information in at least one other encyclopaedia or book to see if it adds anything extra. Figure 6.17 summarises CD ROM 'dos and don'ts'.

FIGURE 6.17 *CD ROM dos and don'ts*

- **DO NOT PASTE INFORMATION STRAIGHT INTO YOUR WORK**
- **DO RE-WRITE INFORMATION IN YOUR OWN WORDS**
- **ALWAYS 'QUOTE YOUR SOURCE'**
- **ALWAYS CHECK THE INFORMATION IN AT LEAST ONE OTHER BOOK**

W O R K S H O P

To put information into your own words you need a set of questions to answer. In this example, a set of questions is given to help you find out about **global warming** from a CD ROM encyclopaedia.

1 Write a report about global warming. Use a CD ROM encyclopaedia. Set your report out using these questions as sub-headings:

a) What is global warming?

b) Why is it happening?

c) What sort of problems is it causing?

d) Which parts of the world will be most affected if global warming continues?

e) Will **MEDCs** be able to cope better with global warming than **LEDCs**? Explain your answer.

f) Is there anything we could do to stop global warming? Has anything been done yet?

g) What do you think we should do about global warming? Give reasons for your opinion.

If you are not given a set of questions to answer, you must come up with your own. The questions in Figure 6.18 will get you started. You do not have to answer all questions for all topics.

FIGURE 6.18 *Enquiry questions for CD ROM investigations*

✳ *What? (What is it that you have been asked to find out about?)*

✳ *Where? (Where is it?)*

✳ *What is it like? (Describe it.)*

✳ *How did it get like that? (Explain it.)*

✳ *Who is affected by it? (Does it cause problems, or bring advantages for anyone?)*

✳ *What can be done about it? (How could it be managed?)*

✳ *How is it likely to change? (What will it be like in the future?)*

✳ *What do you think should happen? (What is your opinion?)*

W O R D   B O X

global warming the temperature of the atmosphere rising

LEDCs Less Economically Developed Countries: the poorer countries of, mainly, South America, Africa and Asia

MEDCs More Economically Developed Countries: the richer countries of, mainly, North America and Europe

6.7 *Using the Internet*

Internet 1

Introduction

The Internet is a way of linking together computers anywhere in the world. If two computers are on the Internet then they can get in touch with each other. This means that you can get information from a computer in Kenya, Australia or the USA. Each piece of information has an address. To 'dial up' an address you have to follow a number of steps, which are the same for all computers. Figure 6.19 shows the stages you would have to go through to connect to a **website** with information about the rainforest.

FIGURE 6.19 *Logging on to an Internet address*

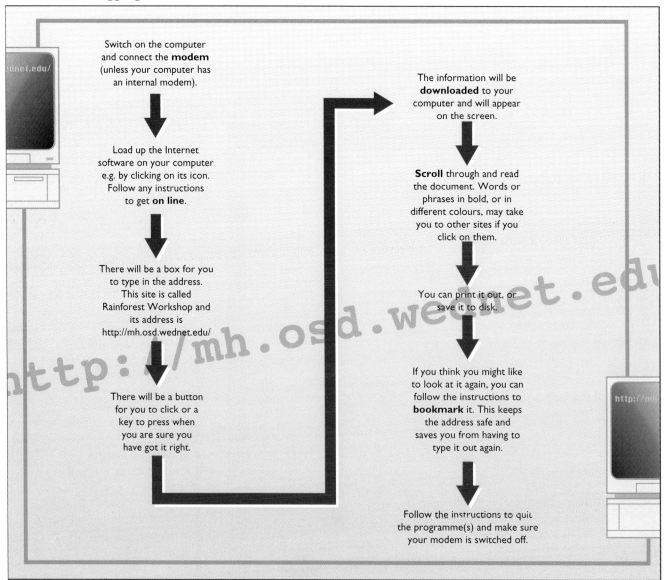

Switch on the computer and connect the **modem** (unless your computer has an internal modem).

Load up the Internet software on your computer e.g. by clicking on its icon. Follow any instructions to get **on line**.

There will be a box for you to type in the address. This site is called Rainforest Workshop and its address is http://mh.osd.wednet.edu/

There will be a button for you to click or a key to press when you are sure you have got it right.

The information will be **downloaded** to your computer and will appear on the screen.

Scroll through and read the document. Words or phrases in bold, or in different colours, may take you to other sites if you click on them.

You can print it out, or save it to disk.

If you think you might like to look at it again, you can follow the instructions to **bookmark** it. This keeps the address safe and saves you from having to type it out again.

Follow the instructions to quit the programme(s) and make sure your modem is switched off.

1 a) 'Dial up' the Rainforest Workshop in Figure 6.19.
   b) Write a brief description of what the site is about.
   c) Write down five pieces of information that you have learnt from
       the site.
   d) Bookmark it for future reference.
2 a) Choose one of the sites from the list in Figure 6.20. Between
       them they cover the main themes studied in geography.
   b) Dial it up.
   c) Write down what it is about.
   d) Write down five pieces of information that you have learnt from
       the site.
   e) Bookmark it.
   f) Compare it with the Rainforest Workshop site. Which site did
       you prefer? Why?

Theme	Name	Address
earthquakes	Museum of the City of San Francisco	http:www.sfmuseum.org
volcanoes	Cascades Volcano Observatory HOME PAGE	http://vulcan.wr.usgs.gov/home.html
rivers	Institute of Hydrology Home Page	http:www.nwl.ac.uk/ih
coasts	NOAA Central Library	http://www.lib.noaa.gov
weather and climate	Met Office Home Page	http://www.meto.govt.uk
ecosystems	Rainforest Action Network	http://www.ran.org/ran
population	United Nations POPIN Survey	http:www.undp.org:81/popin
settlement	About Calcutta	http:www.gl.umbc.edu/%7Eachatt1/calcutta.html
economic activities	Global Energy Marketplace	http://gem.crest.org
development	UN Statistics Division Home Page	http:www.un.org/Depts/unsd/social/main.htm
environmental issues	Environmental Database	http://www.soton.ac.uk/~engenvir

FIGURE 6.20 *Internet addresses*

W O R D   B O X

bookmark   adding the Internet address to a special list for future
reference
downloaded   information sent to your computer
modem   the piece of equipment that allows information to be
transferred over a telephone line
on line   this is when you are connected to the Internet
scroll   move up and down the document using (usually) the
arrows at the side of the window
website   the place an Internet address takes you to

Internet 2

Introduction

You do not have to know an Internet address to be able to look up information. You can find out information about almost any topic by using a **search engine** to **browse** or 'surf' the Internet. How to do this is shown in Figure 6.21 and some examples of search engines are given in Figure 6.22. It can take quite a long time to find a really good site. Even then, it is important to **evaluate** the source by answering the questions in Figure 6.23. If you think that there might be different opinions, try to find some other sites about the same topic and compare what they say. When you use the information in your account or project remember the CD ROM 'rules' on page 146.

FIGURE 6.21 *Surfing the Internet*

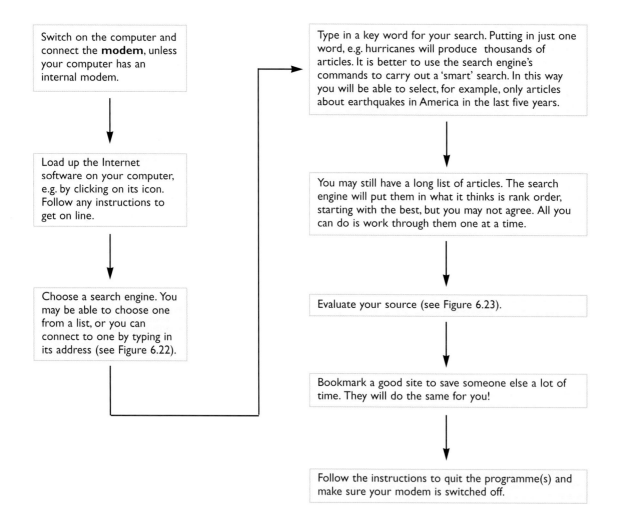

Switch on the computer and connect the **modem**, unless your computer has an internal modem.

Load up the Internet software on your computer, e.g. by clicking on its icon. Follow any instructions to get on line.

Choose a search engine. You may be able to choose one from a list, or you can connect to one by typing in its address (see Figure 6.22).

Type in a key word for your search. Putting in just one word, e.g. hurricanes will produce thousands of articles. It is better to use the search engine's commands to carry out a 'smart' search. In this way you will be able to select, for example, only articles about earthquakes in America in the last five years.

You may still have a long list of articles. The search engine will put them in what it thinks is rank order, starting with the best, but you may not agree. All you can do is work through them one at a time.

Evaluate your source (see Figure 6.23).

Bookmark a good site to save someone else a lot of time. They will do the same for you!

Follow the instructions to quit the programme(s) and make sure your modem is switched off.

FIGURE 6.22   *Search engines*

Name	Address
Alta Vista	http://www.altavista.digital.com
Yahoo!	http://www.yahoo.com
UK Yellow web	http://www.yell.co.uk
Magellan	http:www.mckinley.com

W O R D   B O X

browse   to carry out a search for a particular topic
evaluate   to decide how good and/or reliable the source is
search engine   a huge database of information that is available on the Internet

FIGURE 6.23   *Evaluating an Internet site*

Name of site

Topic

Address

Who was it written by (can they be trusted)?

When was it written (is it up to date)?

What are their main opinions (if any)?

Do I need to check other sites to see if they say the same thing?

W O R K S H O P

1 a) Evaluate the Rainforest Workshop (see page 148) and the Rainforest Action Network (see page 149) sites.
   b) How are the two sites different?
   c) Why do you think this is the case?
2 Use a search engine to browse for information about the most recent topic you have been studying in geography. Try to find out some extra information for your notes. Evaluate your source. Try to answer some of the key geographical questions: Where is it? What is it like? How did it get like that? How is it changing? What will it be like in the future?

6.8 Data loggers

Introduction

Data loggers automatically record data. They will carry on recording for days, months or even longer. The data they collect can be **downloaded** into a computer so that it can be analysed and presented.

Some schools have automatic weather stations like the one in Figure 6.24. These record weather data such as temperature, rainfall and pressure for 60 or more days at a time. The data can be analysed and presented, compared with the daily national forecasts, and compared with the school's **micro-climate**.

Another type of data logger is shown in Figure 6.25. It is battery operated and can be fitted with three electronic sensors. The white leads on this one are measuring temperature while the other sensor is measuring light. Other types of sensors can be fitted as well, e.g. for measuring wind speed. It is controlled by the red and green buttons on the front. Again, when the data has been collected it can be downloaded into a computer for analysis and presentation.

FIGURE 6.24 *Automatic weather recorder*

FIGURE 6.25 *Data logger*

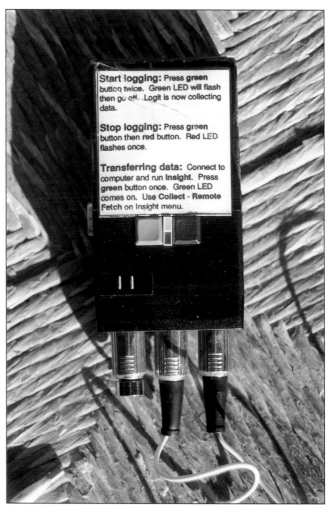

This is a straightforward investigation using a data logger fitted with two temperature sensors and a light sensor.

(a) Aims:
  i) To test the **hypothesis** that soil temperature is lower than air temperature.
  ii) To test the hypothesis that soil temperature changes less than air temperature.

(b) Method: Set up the data logger as shown in Figure 6.26. (Protect it if there is a chance of rain.) Make a note of which sensor is recording soil temperature and which is recording air temperature. Record data for a full 24-hour period. Then, download the data you have collected into your computer.

(c) Presentation, analysis and explanation: On your computer, present the data as a **comparative line graph**. Compare the temperature lines: what do you notice? See if there is a relationship between the light recordings and the temperature recordings. Try to explain your findings.

(d) Evaluation: Did you have any problems with the survey? Are there any ways in which your results might be misleading or inaccurate? How could the investigation be improved and/or developed?

(e) Conclusions: Did you prove or disprove your hypotheses?

FIGURE 6.26 *Setting up the investigation*

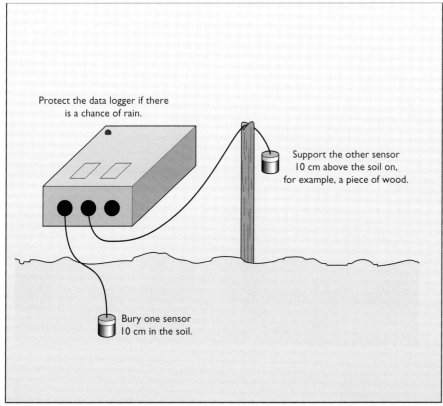

Protect the data logger if there is a chance of rain.

Support the other sensor 10 cm above the soil on, for example, a piece of wood.

Bury one sensor 10 cm in the soil.

WORD BOX

comparative line graph a graph with more than one line drawn on the same graph outline (see pages 10–11)
downloaded information sent to your computer
hypothesis an idea to be tested
micro-climate the climate of a small area caused by local factors

6.9 *E-mail*

Introduction

E-mail (electronic mail) is a way of sending and receiving messages and data from people anywhere in the world, as long as they have a computer and an e-mail address. It is a quick, easy and (once you have paid for the equipment and the connection charges) cheap means of communication. For geographers, it has a particular advantage because you can send photographs and images, and information in the form of a database. It also means that you can get up to date information from far away places.

Sending and getting e-mails is similar to using the Internet. There are different e-mail systems, but they all work in much the same way. The main stages you need to go through are shown in Figure 6.27.

FIGURE 6.27 *Sending and receiving e-mails*

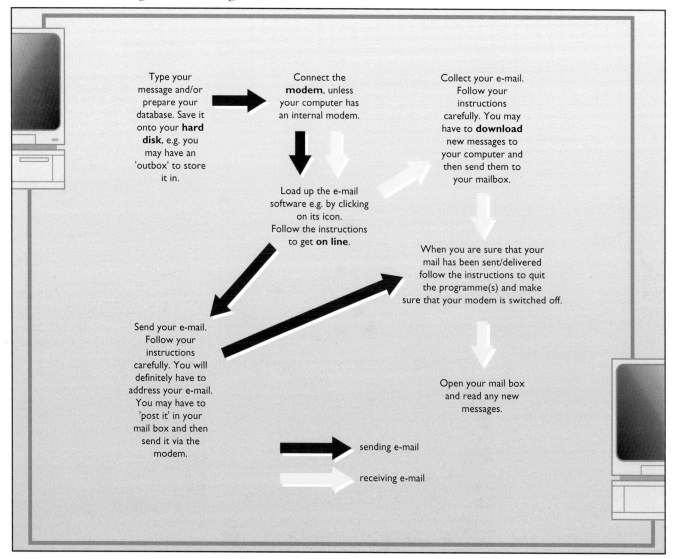

Project 1

This idea involves 'twinning' with a school to set up an e-mail project. It could be a school that you visit on language exchanges, or a school in your town's 'twin town', for example.

(a)   Agree what you are doing to collect information about. (Do this by e-mailing each other.) For example, you could both answer the same questions, such as: Where is our settlement located? What is its population? What are its main industries? How is it changing? What do young people think of it? Alternatively, or as well as, you could agree to collect weather data for the same two weeks: maximum and minimum temperature; rainfall; wind direction; and wind speed. This information could be recorded in a database.

(b)   Agree when you are going to carry out the project.

(c)   Agree who is going to do the work!

(d)   When you have collected the information, e-mail it to your partner.

(e)   Compare your results. Use them as the basis for a major display.

Project 2

This idea involves you in e-mailing your project proposal to **newsgroups** to see if anyone is interested in taking part. You can then choose who you would like to be involved and e-mail them further details.

(a)   Write your project proposal and e-mail it to a number of newsgroups. For example, you could ask for volunteers anywhere in the world to collect weather data (e.g. maximum and minimum temperature; rainfall; wind direction; and wind speed) once a day for a particular week.

(b)   If you get enough replies, decide who you would like to take part (for example, you could try to get an even distribution) and e-mail them details of exactly what they have to do, and when.

(c)   They will e-mail you their data when the collection period is over. You then put it together and e-mail the 'master data' to everyone who took part. You could do this as text, or as a database.

(d)   Each person who took part can then present and analyse the data for themselves.

WORD BOX

download   information sent to your computer
hard disc   the disc drive inside your computer
modem   the piece of equipment that allows information to be transferred over a telephone line
newsgroup   groups of people who have agreed to share information
on line   this is when you are connected to the outside world

Index